SOMETIME BEFORE THE DAWN:

Responses to the Resurrection

by
Richard M. Cromie, D.D., Ph.D.

Desert Ministries Press
Matthews, North Carolina

SOMETIME BEFORE THE DAWN

Second Edition 2007
(First Edition 1982)

Copyright 2007 by
Desert Ministries, Inc.
P.O. Box 747
Matthews, NC 28106
ISBN 0-914733-34-6

Printed by Eagle Graphic Services, Fort Lauderdale, Florida

DEDICATION

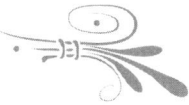

To the memory of

My parents
Harry Marlin and Margaret Acker Cromie
My brother
Robert Harry Cromie
My wife's parents
Melvin Curtis and Catherine Dickson Good
And the myriad of family and dear friends
Who have crossed over to the other side.

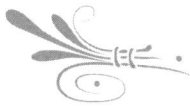

TABLE OF CONTENTS

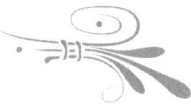

ACKNOWLEDGEMENTS

It has been a long journey to this point, and there are many to thank along the way. My parents, my sisters, Carol and Alice, and my brother Bob got me started looking for all things good. My early teachers, Isobel Sheets and Margaret Morrison, kept me going and were dear to me. Robert P. Newman, my debate coach at Pitt, Gordon E. Jackson at Seminary and James Aiken Whyte at St. Mary's College kept me honest and made me think. Dr. Howard C. Scharfe at Shadyside Church nudged me off the starting line into ministry. Friends and parishioners all along the way shared their lives with me, in good times and other times. Most of what I know I have learned by watching and listening to them. I am not an original thinker. Self-deception is not one of my sins. But I usually recognize truth and a good idea when I hear them. My dear Aunt Mary asked me one day near the end of her life how I learned all the "stuff" I knew. "It sure surprises us, Richie," she said. And like my whole bountiful life, it surprises me too.

For the making of this book, I thank Sandra Steving Green, who typed the original edition and is now a Board Member of DMI; Elinor Bloom Simpson, the first Executive Director of Desert Ministries Inc., who managed the original publication; my wife, Peggy, the current director of DMI, who read through the manuscript and suggested a hundred helpful changes. Our three daughters, Cathie, Cammie and Courtney, deserve more than a nod of gratitude. They and our grandchildren, Maddie and Wil, inspire me and make life worth living.

Carson Overstreet, the Administrative Assistant in our office, typed and retyped this manuscript. I am grateful for that. Holly Strawbridge, who edits all our books, worked her magic on this one as well. J.D. Thrower of Eagle Graphic Services in Fort Lauderdale, a friend and fellow traveler of many years, deserves another vote of appreciation for the layout and printing. Finally, Donna Hudson, a friend here at Sardis Presbyterian Church, gave us the fruits of her professional expertise in editing legal documents and put the fine finishing touches on it all.

Thank you.
Richard M. Cromie
Charlotte, North Carolina
June 30, 2007

PREFACE
TO THIS NEW EDITION

Just as I was finishing this book, the new Billy Graham Library was dedicated here in Charlotte. When I became a Rotary Foundation Fellow in Scotland in 1958, there was much ado and controversy over his Evangelistic Crusade in London. I gladly defended Billy then, and if called upon, I would double my efforts now.

Such bravado is hardly necessary. Billy is loved by all. Intellectual quibbling about born-again Christianity has melded into our tolerance-abundant milieu, where an amalgam of ecumenicity stretches across the variations of Christianity and on into Judaism, Islam, and others faiths. We had better be careful, as Confucius supposedly warned, and not keep our minds so open that our brains will fall out! Tolerance is a virtue, but it is a luxury when things begin to matter. Anyway, Billy is a revered elder statesman and a pastor to the nation. We all share in his loss in the recent death of his wife, Ruth.

Franklin Graham, Billy's son and heir to his ministry, pointed out at the dedication that the Library has one huge front entrance formed in the shape of a Cross. "The only way in is to come through the foot of the cross of Jesus Christ. That has always been my father's message, and we symbolize it here," he said. Through the years, the Graham message has remained the same, and probably will not change. However in our multi-cultural world and the dangers of the times we live in, the Lord might be calling us to a combined effort of all religions to work together for good. We had better learn to hold hands and pull together, or we could end up with no future at all on earth. I would never ask a fellow Christian to tone down what he deeply believes, but radically aggressive Christianity can be almost as harmful as radical Islam.

Not to appear disrespectful, but the conservative stance regarding the inerrant wording of God's Word has never been the cornerstone of my own use of Scripture. I have been led to a larger and more encompassing view, one that honors the Old and New Testaments as the unique and final Word of God, but that also includes the sanctity of the Holy Books of other faiths. For example, I recently re-read the entire <u>Quran</u>, the Islamic Scriptures, so that I could have a more informed understanding of the nearly one billion Muslims in the world. I continue to study Jewish-Christian Literature and follow cross-cultural religious studies. I try to live by the New and Old Testament Scriptures of my faith, but I do not use The Bible to save myself and condemn others. I no longer waste time defending my stance on the Bible, and surely the Bible can take care of itself.

My devotion to Jesus Christ did not arise out of a sense of sin and depravation. I have never felt like a sinner in the hands of an angry God, dangling over the eternal fires of hell. Fact is that I have never felt alienated from the Lord at all. My 1970s answer to the question, "Have you found Jesus?" is still the same: "I never lost him." I have always been a Christian. I was reared in a committed home. My parents not only ushered us to church and to youth groups galore, but they showed us through their lives how Christ intended his people to live and be. When Ruth Bell Graham's sister, Rosa Montgomery, spoke during Ruth's memorial service at Montreat, NC., she noted that she once asked Ruth when she had met the Lord. Ruth replied, "I can't ever remember not knowing Jesus." Neither can I. Some tell us to find Jesus in an instant; others remind us that one does not need to have a bright, shining, emotional born-again moment to be a special friend of the Savior.

Some feel the need for an abrupt reversal and denial of their early religious training. They ask Jesus to come into their hearts to drive out the demons and to fill up the emptiness. That is fine with me, but my heart was never empty. Some feel the need to be washed in the blood of the lamb and label others who disagree as dark and unclean sinners. I am always suspicious of those who pretend to know too much.

My fortune has never changed. Of course, I have had my share of lonely moments and temporary confusion, but neither ever dominated my life. I have lived all my years surrounded by the love of God in Jesus Christ. I go forward in the sure and certain confidence that my earthly walk with Jesus will continue on into all that "forever" means, not because I am good, but because I belong to him. The Lord has never been a stranger to me.

I was baptized as an infant, as was the custom of our family's United Presbyterian faith, and it took. I could never deny the efficacy of that sacramental moment, which my parents chose for me. I was confirmed in the eighth grade by the elders of the Fourth United Presbyterian Church in a brief ceremony I still remember. I recall giggling some, but I also grasped the importance of what was happening right from the start. You might say that I have lived happily ever after.

On an evening long ago, I went forward during a

Presbyterian Youth Rally in Long Beach, California, where Don Moomaw was preaching. My trip down the aisle was not taken to escape my sinful past. Neither was it to pick up my personal ticket to heaven; I already had that in my pocket. I affirm the authenticity of that evening and I see it as a stepping stone in my faith. Mainly though, I recall it as the way the Lord directed me from the other vocational paths I was considering and forced me to focus my attention on full-time ministry.

Thankfully, I had the sense to listen and eventually become a parish minister—still in my mind, a noble profession and the highest calling of all. I love being a pastor and preacher. I tease people that I get paid for doing exactly what I am supposed to do. Now and again I thought about teaching or taking a college or seminary presidency, but whenever that idea visited me, my love of the local church drove it away. Wycliffe translated one of the Old Testament heroes as saying, "I am a lucky fellow." Indeed I am, too.

As my personal faith journey unfolded, there were also some significant changes taking place in the Church and theology that affected my "Responses to the Resurrection." Before we proceed, let me document some of those as they relate to our topic.

I. First, the changes in the American Church. The current attitudes and approaches to the organized church have departed from those of traditional local congregations. For a century, denominational churches—Methodist, Baptist, Episcopal, Roman Catholic, Presbyterian and others—flourished across the land. It was not uncommon to find three or four congregations at the crossroads of a downtown street. In one Pennsylvania town, two huge Presbyterian Churches stood side by side—one United, one not. Those institutional meeting places were often the focal point of the community's agenda. The pastor and the people from their pews were known about town.

But new times came to America, and they also came to churches. Changing communities, social discontent, new highway systems, the urban exodus, our slow response to the needs of those around us, all resulted in membership decline, re-entrenchment and even bewilderment. All traditional denominations, including the Roman Catholic, have experienced severe declines in membership over the past decades. People moved on, and the traditional churches were left behind.

The current outcome of this phenomenon has caused some observers to comment that we have entered a "post-Christian era". I have never adopted that phrase. A good case can be made for a "post-modern time"; but we are nowhere near a post-Christian era. In John Hall's book, <u>The End of Christendom and The Beginning of Christianity</u>, he explains that the life cycle of congregations tends to run a circular course from bad to good and back around again. In these recent years, it has looked like all movement is backwards. However, I think the heart of the faith is being uncovered to prepare it for the future. It is taking a new shape, which is a threat to many, but it is the God Who Acts driving this plan.

While most of traditional churches are still around, they are more often half-empty than full. Some, of course, are gone now. I will never forget the sadness I felt when I watched bull-dozers push down the little church I attended as a youth. Others church buildings are being used as restaurants, antique shops, real estate and law offices, private schools, private homes, and in at least one case, a funeral home.

In <u>Transforming Congregational Culture</u>, Anthony Robinson writes about our new times. For several decades, no matter what church leaders have proposed, the problem has gotten worse. New expressions of the faith have poached church members and stolen them away. Other parishioners have realigned their spiritual fortunes to determine what they need beyond what the local congregation offers. "Old model" churches (as Aubrey Malphurs calls them in his book, <u>A New Kind of Church)</u> are not measuring up. People are not looking for the same answers being reissued by the congregations of our fathers and grandfathers. Demographic trends show that we have moved from small towns to huge metropolitan areas, and mega-churches have followed. Like it or not, it seems to be the American way.

Some new churches resemble massive, sprawling cultural centers, with adjacent theatres and playing fields. They focus less on the historical connections of Calvin, Luther and Wesley, and more on being Christian outposts with a multitude of ministries for their members and people around the world. Some seem to thrive in a conservative-evangelical atmosphere. All seem to have found a way to activate their members to local, national and international mission. And in the uncertainties of recent decades they tend to offer sure and certain articles of faith to hold on to. We all need something to believe in.

Ever since alternative lifestyles have barged onto center stage, it should surprise no one that denominationally minded congregations consisting predominantly of one race or one lifestyle have been moved out of the mainstream of national religious life. Across the nation, many churches are struggling to stay alive. Others of course are growing; but whatever label is affixed to the sign board, they tend to succeed in proportion to the way they move beyond the old denominational approach.

Some denominational churches continue to fuss over what seems to be required in their favorite Bible passages. Others dwell on a particular way of celebrating the Sacraments. Some are intent on excluding people who differ. Others require selected rules and the acceptable kind of good looking people, à la Garrison Keillor, with above average children. They are not gone and forgotten; they are just no longer the mainstream of Christianity. We do seem to be living in a post-denominational age.

In some small towns the problem is easier to identify, but impossible to solve. There are not enough people around to occupy the pews or to form an official quorum when the church council convenes. We used to tell the story of a Bishop who, when he called his young Methodist pastor to learn how things were going in Smithville, was told: "Well, we are not doing very well down here, but thank the good Lord, none of the other churches are doing very well either!"

One of the thorniest problems we face as denominations is how to handle the hurt and anger of the few remaining old-time members who will do anything to keep their church doors open. Our largest waste of the Lord's resources is maintaining the upkeep of buildings we neither use nor need. We need a resurrection, not of the churches, but, as Emil Brunner distinguished, "of The Church". Change appears first in our local churches.

II. The second area of change that affects our understanding of the death and resurrection of Jesus comes from an array of theologians and the new ideas they bring to the topic. They have offered changing theological interpretations of what happened on Calvary, why Jesus had to die a punishing death to gain eternity for his followers, and how the resurrection of our Lord contributes to God's gift of eternal life.

The Doctrine of the Atonement, which is the essence of Christianity, has always stated that Jesus died to save us from our sins. Sure enough he did. But what does that statement actually mean? How could a loving God require the brutal death of his only Son? Traditional answers offer that the justice of a righteous God required that some payment should be made to assuage the offended Creator. Otherwise, the guilty children would get forgiveness for free. I have never found that answer to be entirely satisfactory, but it surely does not satisfy the rising young theologians who challenge the concept of a God who would participate in violence to expiate the sins of violent children. The Penal Theory of the Atonement is being questioned.

Starting with St. Anselm in the 11th century, the church has officially believed that the death of Christ was a ransom paid to God. It took the death of his perfect son to mollify God's anger and to make all his human beings One again with the Creator. Nothing short of that could win salvation for the fallen men and women of the world.

A half-century later, Abelard offered a different view in his Moral Influence Theory, which said, in short, that when Christians see the love of God that allowed his son to die, they would look up to him and be moved to follow in his footsteps.

The Reformers, especially Calvin and Melanchthon, followed Thomas Aquinas in what is called The Substitutionary Atonement. This theory believes Jesus of Nazareth paid the price as a substitute for each of us. In other words, he literally served our death sentences.

Other variations on those theories exist. But the average Christian, when asked what it means to say that Christ died for our sins, will answer to the effect that Jesus died instead of each of me; he took my place. As a result, God does not look at my sin, but he looks at me and sees Jesus. My debt is forgiven; I am at One with God again. As familiar as that sounds, our redemption is attained out of the violence of a God who cannot forgive his children without demanding the sacrifice of Jesus. The perfect Lamb needs to be sacrificed on the altar of the Cross, and the Lamb of God is Jesus, his only son.

Violence in the traditional atonement studies is bothersome to theologians such as Professor Robin Collins, a Mennonite Scholar. In <u>Understanding Atonement: A New and Orthodox Theory</u>, he refuses to locate our forgiveness in the punishment of Jesus. He proposes that our role as Christians is to become immersed in the life of Jesus, to become more like him, to be joined in the willingness to suffer for others and even to die for our beliefs. That way, our sins will be forgiven.

Authors writing from the African-American and feminist points of view move further away from the violence theories. For example, in <u>Proverbs of Ashes</u> Rita Brock and Rebecca Parker emphasize how violence, power and the abuse of humans are acute enough without such heavenly violence and "the ultimate child abuse" on the Son of God. They turn their backs on traditional views of atonement. They conclude that the redemptive process begins when we identify with the suffering of Jesus as he hangs helpless on the cross, which then inspires those who love him to go out and change this violent and abusive world.

In, <u>The Nonviolent Atonement</u>, J. Denny Weaver restates the old Christus Victor theory of Gustav Aulen, which opposes the violent theories of debts paid for sin and sacrifices to assuage either an angry God or the devil. He sees the death of Christ as a victory over the principalities and powers of this mortal life. Jesus mastered life where everyone else had failed. With this theory, our salvation comes not out of one death on one cross long ago, but it comes in a continuous story that began at Calvary and adds another chapter each time we manage to conquer the same principalities and powers of sin and human degradation. If we share in his suffering, we will also share his victory.

While I have profited greatly in my own thinking about the death of Jesus by reading these theologians, I cannot accept all of their conclusions. Exactly how we were put at One again with God by the death of Jesus on the cross remains unsettled. While those authors I mention do not agree in all detail, they are united that the "violence" of traditional views of the atonement are not suited to the mindset of the 21st Century. I am content to say that the death of Jesus on the Cross is the means by which salvation is offered. The death occurred. As John Calvin advised on another issue, it is not good for us to inquire too completely as to what God has in mind. "My ways are not your ways," said the Lord.

III. In addition to these recent inquiries into the sacrificial death of Jesus, there has been increasing scholarly and public interest regarding the resurrection of the body of Jesus. From the beginning, there has been argument concerning what exactly happened when Jesus was raised from the dead; with what kind of body did he come? The Gospel records themselves are not clear. At times the Risen Christ seems to take the form of a spirit, which prompts many to postulate a spiritual resurrection. He walks through doors, disappears without warning and appears mysteriously in an instant. The disciples on the Road to Emmaus did not recognize him, and he told Mary not to touch him, for he had not yet ascended to the Father.

At other times he appears to be in fully human form. Jesus did tell Mary not to touch him, but in John and Luke he encouraged the disciples, especially Thomas, to touch his hands and side to prove that he was really there. He sat down to eat a meal with the disciples, and Luke tells us that Jesus ate the food. (Luke 24:43)

It also seems from the texts that the disciples themselves were not entirely sure of what had happened. It is obvious they were not conspiring with each other to tell a consistent story. Matthew is honest in reporting that when the 11 disciples went out to the mountain in Galilee, "When they saw him they worshipped him, but some doubted" (Matthew 28:17).

Little wonder that controversy has existed over whether the risen body was a physical body or a spiritual one. We were taught in Seminary to defend the physical resurrection as the one essential truth of what happened on Easter morning. Over the years, I have been asked by young and old alike if I really believed in it, implying that it was too incredible for an intelligent person to accept.

The whole matter has returned in theological studies of the last quarter of a century. Scholars and writers from both sides of the theological aisle have explained how it could or could not have been. In an excellent article in the Journal for the Study of the Historical Jesus, 2005, Vol. 3.2, New Testament scholar Gary R. Habermas surveys recent scholarly publications on the birth, death and resurrection of Jesus. No less than 1,400 important works have been published in the past 25 years. He organizes the works into the conservative, the skeptical and what he calls "moderate conservatism." This camp believes that Jesus was actually raised from the dead in some physical or spiritual body. Others deny the verity of the Gospel stories completely.

Recent trends, Habermas writes, include "naturalistic explanations" such as subjective visions, hallucinations, wish-fulfilling projections—all of which are states of mind. Some scholars reject the physical resurrection as a historical event at all. John Crossan, for example, believes that the resurrection was only a metaphor to indicate what God was trying to accomplish. All agree that it is difficult to decipher what went on inside and outside the Garden tomb.

There can be no doubt that the earliest Christians who reported Jesus's appearances after his death took these events to be real. Their belief in the resurrection is indisputable. Reginald Fuller postulates, as Dibelius had before him, that if the resurrection is not accepted as physical and real, some other "X" factor must be offered to account for what they saw and heard, which prompted them to move forward.

Not only do we have the Gospel narratives of Easter morning, but we also have the testimony of St. Paul as to the post-resurrection appearances of the Lord. In I Corinthians 15, Paul enumerates a number of appearances: "Jesus appeared to Cephas, then to the twelve. Then he appeared to more than 500 brethren at one time, most of whom are still alive, although some have fallen asleep. Then he appeared to James, then to all of the apostles. Last of all, as to one untimely born, he appeared also to me." From Acts 9, it seems certain that the appearance to Paul was a "spiritual" one: he heard, but did not see, the presence of Christ.

It can be assumed that Paul received additional information from Simon Peter and James, the brother of Jesus. He tells in Galatians 1 about how he went to Jerusalem "after three years" and spent 15 days with Cephas. The three years after his conversion would date his visit to the middle-to-late years of the third decade, say 36 to 39 C.E. The testimony they shared with him would have been as fresh as three, four to six years following the death of Jesus. In the memory of so astounding an event, a few years is a proverbial drop in the bucket. When critics tout that the Gospels were not written down for 30 to 70 years after the event, thereby creating suspicion that their memories were faulty, they would not explain away St. Paul, who received his information from eyewitnesses just a few short years after the death and resurrection of the Lord.

Something wondrous happened to the friends, family and followers of Jesus which injected a new enthusiasm into their fallen hopes. It came from God, to be sure, and it took root in their conviction that Jesus Christ was risen from the dead. Their rebirth in spirit and soul cannot be denied. Their first Easter and the Resurrection appearances that followed gave them the courage to go on.

IV. Other discoveries from "New Testament times". While various non-canonical books and fragments concerning the life and teaching of Jesus and his followers have long been known, just after World War II an Arab peasant made an astonishing accidental discovery of some long hidden apocryphal "Gnostic Gospels". The old scrolls and fragments were found inside a red earthenware jar in a cave near the town of Nag Hammadi in Upper Egypt. These are not the more widely known Dead Sea Scrolls, even though the accidental discovery is similar. These documents refer to New Testament times and people, not as the Scrolls, to the Old Testament. Pity was that he did not know what he had found. Some of them were subsequently burned as fuel by his mother to warm their modest hut. But what remained, added to several other discoveries, has cast a new searchlight on how the good news of Christ developed into the theology of the Church.

The 52 manuscripts from what is called The Nag Hammadi Library are spoken of casually by many seminarians, lay persons and clergy. They are accepted as interesting and even worthy of a second look. But, to many Pastors and most lay people in the pews, they are relegated to incidental importance, if known at all, and thought to be largely heretical and misleading.

However sixty years after their discovery it is certain to those who study the collection that they offer a monumental break-through in New Testament studies, much like the Dead Sea Scrolls does with some of the Old Testament.

More importantly for us in this book, they have brought new information and interest in the death and resurrection of Jesus. Just within the past year another new flurry of papers and books has been published offering a broadened understanding of the Biblical texts. I recommend the single volume discussion by James M. Robinson, <u>The Nag Hamada Library,</u> for a complete study.

There are others. The newly released: <u>Reading Judas</u>: <u>The</u>
<u>Gospel of Judas and the Shaping of Christianity</u>, written by
Elaine Pagels, at Princeton (an old favorite of mine) and Karen
L. King of Harvard Divinity School, inserts a scholarly if con-
troversial reflection on Judas Iscariot. Continuing their careful
and scholarly work in the field of the Apocryphal and Gnostic
Gospels, the authors explain how helpful this non-canonical
book is in understanding how Christianity developed. It is
purported to have been written by Judas Iscariot, the disciple
who betrayed Jesus; but that does not seem to be possible for it
is certain that The Gospel of Judas was not written until a century after the disciple who betrayed Jesus in the Gospels would
have died. While this "Gospel" is casually discarded by many,
it still can be helpful in understanding what the Bible says and
what happened in the death and resurrection of Jesus.

In her much earlier book, <u>The Gnostic Gospels</u>, (1979)
Professor Pagels wrote about the importance of the other non-
canonical gospel materials in framing the details of the resurrection story. Some of these non-Biblical "gospels" add inci-
dents and details to the first Easter story; including, for our
purposes, the controversies Christians have on what kind of
"body" was raised to life again after Jesus died. In the New
Testament time itself and in the decades following, there seems
to have been divergent views over whether the body was a physical or spiritual presence. As we will mention in more detail
later, there was confusion about what the risen "body"
appeared to be to those who saw the resurrected Jesus. At times
they did not recognize the Risen Christ; at other times they
know exactly who He was. Sometimes they experienced a vir-
tual body, a "heavenly body", e.g., when Jesus told Mary not to
touch him in the garden outside the Tomb.

At other times, such as Luke 24: 36-43, Jesus told the disciples that he was real live flesh and blood. He asked them for something to eat and "they gave him a piece of broiled fish and he ate it." He added: "Handle me, and see; for a spirit has not flesh and bones as you see I have." (Luke 23: 39)

To the contrary, When St. Paul discussed the resurrected body, he wrote clearly in I Corinthians 15: "It is sown a physical body, it is raised a spiritual body." (15: 44); and "I tell you this, brethren: flesh and blood cannot inherit the kingdom of God, nor does the perishable inherit the imperishable." (15: 50)

In the Epistle Apostolorum, a much later letter, purported to have been written by the eleven remaining disciples to the Christians of the world, there are some additional conversations with the Risen Lord which do not appear in the Four Gospels, as well as comment on other times in the life they shared with Jesus. (Hennecke, New Testament Apocrypha, Volume I, pp.188ff.) There Jesus invited Peter and Andrew, as well as Thomas, to touch the nail prints in his hands and side. Jesus also pointed to the indentation which his foot made in the ground, and told them that ghosts do not leave footprints in the sand.

The New Testament contains a variety of opinions on this and other subjects. How then should we reconcile the two views and other possible insights from the non-canonical gospels?

In the first place, some of the additional details put forward are fascinating, as they try to include details of the story which are not present in the Four Gospels. In the Gospel of Mary, which is purported to have been written by Mary Magdalene, there is mention that Mary was selected by Jesus to share special and secret conversations. This is part of the background which has brought some to speculate that Mary and Jesus were intimates. There is a remarkable scene in the Gospel of Mary where Mary returned from the Tomb on the first Easter morning and told the disciples that she had seen Jesus. Of course they do not believe her, as our New Testament says the disciples did not believe the women. But the Gospel of Mary adds a discussion which took place among the disciples. Andrew and Simon Peter told her they did not believe her, implying that she was an emotional woman. Then Levi (Matthew) spoke up in her defense and tried to vindicate her. (New Testament Apocrypha, Edgar Hennecke, Volume I, p. 343.) We cannot be sure if the reported incident is true or not. Surely the Four Gospels do not pretend to exhaust all possible stories about the post-resurrection period. But in this case it seems to be a deliberate attempt to elevate the position of Mary in the early church.

The Gospel of Peter also adds some detail to what the Four Gospels tell us of the resurrection. Here a huge crowd came out of Jerusalem and from the outlying country to see the empty sepulcher. It is not mentioned in the Gospel of Peter that Jesus appeared to the crowd, but there could be a veiled reference here to the time St. Paul notes that Jesus had appeared to 500 people, most of whom are still alive. (I Corinthians 15: 6) Through the night before, Peter adds that two soldiers on guard heard a loud voice from heaven and saw two men descending. They awakened the Centurion and the elders who were sleeping nearby, keeping watch. The stone, engagingly, rolled itself away. The two men went into the tomb. A short while later three men came out, the one in the middle, presumably Jesus, was sustained by the other two. Curiously, a cross walked under its own power behind them. Then the heavens opened a second time and another man came down. His appearance prompted the Centurion and the guards to go down and tell Pilate that this was truly the Son of God. Pilate commanded them to tell no one, in fear that his followers and others soon to be converted would create a rebellion against his rule, or at least spoil his desire for a promotion. (Ibid. Volume I, p. 185-187.)

In the <u>Gospel of Peter</u>, Mary Magdalene came to the tomb with her woman friends, wondering about the stone. This re-telling of the story brings Mary (alone in John) and the others from the Synoptic Gospels together. The tomb had already been opened. They saw a young man seated there in a bright and shining robe. He told them he was risen, "Come see where he used to be." As it is also told in Mark, "The women fled, affrighted." (Peter 1:7)

(Note: the best single source of most of the non-canonical materials is a two-volume book, <u>New Testament Apocrypha</u>, edited by Edgar Hennecke, which is included in the bibliography at the end of this book. A more contemporary coverage is found in Bart D. Ehrman's <u>Lost Scriptures</u>. Others write ably about the subject, but for the actual texts themselves I still rely on the Hennecke volume because it is good, but also because it was translated by a friend of mine, Professor Robin McL. Wilson, of St. Mary's College at the University of St. Andrews, Scotland)

In mentioning these "gospels" I do not mean to elevate them to the level of Scripture and I do not even hint that they could be rivals to the material in the four canonized Gospels of Matthew, Mark, Luke and John.

What I intend is to show is that it was a curious route to the adoption of an official New Testament Gospel, during which all the possible claimants, other than the Four, were excluded. The selective process does not appear to be as pure and objective and heaven-sent as one might first assume.

There were many competing and conflicting manuscripts in circulation at the time. Some differed in historical details but also in theological intent. The pluralism of theological ideas then was no less real that it is today. But there was no way to settle arguments as to what the Bible said. Some way had to be found to adopt an official record of what happened in the life, death and resurrection of Jesus. Which would be the approved biography as we would call it in our time? Disagreements would continue, but at least there is/was some kind of official word to measure the arguments against.

To drop back: most committed Christians in our time tend to assume that the 27 books of the New Testament have always been our sacred irreplaceable Scriptures, as if they were deposited directly from on high into the hands of the early church. After all we say they are "authorized" and inspired. The riveted opinion that these were somehow dictated into the souls and psyches of the apostles by the Spirit of God is an enduring one. My first Bible teacher in college told us they were "Authorized", a word it turns out he found on the opening page of the venerable King James Bible, where it means only that King James VI authorized them to be read in the 17th Century churches of Great Britain.

That conviction has eased some in the decades of my ministry, but there remains an assumption that the authorized words of the Creator were written down in final English form and locked up forever in our chosen New Testament. That way the Church can feel secure knowing that we have in our hands the exclusive scoop on what God had to say. I mean no disrespect of the Scripture, nor do I wish to challenge its faithful adherents. But an unsupported declaration that what we read in the Bible is meant to be taken literally as translated in the chosen edition is still a formidable foe to those who seek to understand how and when and why the "Bible" came to be.

The Bible is the inspired word of God to me. But even a cursory look at how the final New Testament developed requires a careful examination of the haphazard route taken along the way. The Canon, the approved books of the Bible, was not miraculously deposited with the early Church Fathers the day after Jesus ascended into heaven; nor even in the immediate years and decades to follow. While some of Paul's New Testament letters were written around 50 AD, or CE if you prefer, it was not until the very last part of the 4th Century that some semblance of the canon as we now have it was accepted. And still then, it was not universally agreed by all the Christian Churches.

Prior to that time, in a history of the development of the New Testament wonderfully told by Professor Bruce Metzgar in The Canon of the New Testament, there was "a long and gradual progress" which lingered for more than three centuries. There is also a more recent study of The Biblical Canon by Canadian scholar Lee Martin McDonald. The latter includes information on how the Old Testament Canon was similarly developed. Both of these authors agree that the process of selecting the final New Testament books was worked out in compromise and common consent along the way.

This is not the appropriate time or place to digress into a lengthy dissertation of how the Bible came to be. Endless volumes have been published on that subject through the centuries. We do not have time or space to do so, nor is it within the stated boundaries of this book.

However, if our chosen New Testament canon is sacrosanct and untouchable, we should at least be aware that there were other letters and studies of Jesus which might have been included. A few almost were. <u>The Codex Sinaiticus,</u> the oldest extant Christian Bible, from the Fourth Century AD, includes all 66 books (but in a different order from our Bible), plus some apocryphal books of the Old Testament period. And then, appended to the New Testament, are <u>The Epistle of Barnabas</u> and the <u>Shepherd of Hermas</u>, two widely known Christian writings at the time. It appears that they were being treated as God's word. Here and there in the early church other gospels and letters were treated as Scripture and read as Holy Writ in the gatherings of the church. And, even where they were not, they can still help us to interpret the gospel records that we now have.

For many generations there was a growing agreement on what subject matter was reliable, both in historical and theological terms, but it was not until 367 A.D. when Athanasius, the Bishop of Alexandria, advised the Christians in Egypt under his jurisdiction to accept the 39 books we now have as the Old Testament, and the 27 we now accept as the New. This was the first more or less official declaration on the topic. He told them that no other books should be added to his list. But, like good thinking Christians everywhere, only some of his flock listened and obeyed. The vociferous debates which surrounded the subject for over the three previous centuries continued to echo long after his advice was given.

Prior to that time there were attempts to codify some selected writings of the stories and teachings of Jesus of Nazareth. In his book <u>Lost Scriptures</u>; Professor Bart Ehrman introduces us to several previous "canons" (pp. 330 ff.). Dozens, if not hundreds of early Christian writings were considered. Someone in authority had to declare officially what the truth of the matter really was. The wide fluctuations in what these apocryphal gospels attributed to Jesus and his closest followers caused continual dissension. For a couple of centuries this faction and that came up with its own "scriptural justification" and the written documents to prove they were right.

Augustine the famous Bishop of Hippo in North Africa ratified the Athanasian suggestion of the 27 New Testament books at a Synod meeting in 393. Still the approved scriptures continued to differ in the Western and the Eastern churches. As a matter of fact, as most Christians know, the Roman Catholic and Protestant Bibles in the Western World still are not identical today. Some areas of the faith held on to their own selections of good and holy writ.

The Church Fathers in Syria and Ethiopia, for example, advocated varying texts. The Shepherd of Hermas, The Epistle of Barnabas, and the Gospel of Thomas and others were suggested for possible inclusion. As late as the Reformation the arguments continued. While there was widespread agreement on the Four Gospels, and while it was included it in his New Testament translation, at one fiery moment Martin Luther declared that the Book of James was not worthy to wrap his rubbish in.

In the mid 16th Century the Council of Trent solidified the Roman Catholic Canon, as we have it today. The various Protestant denominations followed with theirs, largely omitting the Old Testament Apocryphal Books which were included in the approved Roman Catholic Bible. Some chose to rearrange the materials to suit their own doctrinal persuasion.

Back in the early Third Century AD, the noted Origen separated the enormous pile of "gospels" into categories from "acceptable to disputed to spurious to heretical". At times the additional material is intriguing. Many of the sayings of Jesus in the <u>Gospel of Thomas,</u> for example, sound much like the Four Gospels themselves. The <u>Shepherd of Hermas</u> is worth a good read, as is the <u>Didache,</u> and the <u>Infancy Gospels</u>. Details of the birth and childhood of Jesus in some of the Infancy Gospels are fascinating, even endearing at times.

However the disputes were not always idle or incidental. For example, some of these spurious "gospels" were absolutely heretical, on purpose. They taught that Jesus was not really God incarnate. He was a good person with good ideas, not unlike what many would write today. To some he was less than "fully God"; while with others he was less than fully man. He masqueraded around as a man, but underneath he was still in his spiritual body. He never died a human death at all; he just appeared to be dead. When he arose from the grave he came out of a deep trance. The ramifications of that kind of incarnation would remove all that we believe Jesus was and did. Some official pronouncement was necessary as to what could and should be accepted as Gospel Truth.

Pagels and Ehrman and many others who research and write in this area do not reject the Canon of the New Testament. Nor are they trying to persuade the Church to include some these other writings. But a careful look at what other doctrines were believed and the "gospel" authority to defend them, tell us a great deal more of what the early church believed and how it came to finalize the books of the Bible.

V. The final contemporary concern I will mention arises out of the flurry of recent archeological discoveries and speculation surrounding the body of Jesus. From the beginning, the Church has never been explicit in declaring what happened to the body of our Lord after he was raised. We might also ask similarly what happened to the body of Lazarus, who in John 11 was resurrected from death. Did Lazarus face death again, or did some apotheosis take him up to heaven at the end of his life? With Lazarus, this becomes an academic discussion. With Jesus Christ, the answer has far-reaching consequences. If you believe in the resurrection of the physical body of Jesus, then the body has to go somewhere other than back into the grave. The ascension is critical to understanding what happened.

Our age is not the first to ponder this matter. Throughout the centuries a variety of theories have been put forward by friends and foes alike. Some have said that Jesus only appeared to be dead, but he was really in a catatonic state brought on by the heat of the Palestinian sun. When he was placed in a cool shady grave, he quietly came back to life. But Mark tells how Pilate questioned the centurion to make sure he was dead, and the centurion reported that he was (Mark 15:44-45). Some said that the body was stolen, or removed by friends to make sure it would not be stolen. Others who accept a spiritual resurrection have even speculated that the women went to the wrong tomb, and not finding the body there, they were surprised by a vision of Jesus.

The most threatening recent proposal has been made by some well-known archeologists and Biblical scholars who recently shared the secret that they have discovered the tomb in which Jesus is buried. Back in the 1980s, some ancient tombs were unearthed during the construction of a new apartment in a Jerusalem building complex. Armed with state-of-the-art archeological tools, including DNA analysis, they descended into the tomb, where they found their evidence.

James Cameron, a successful motion picture director, made a television documentary about this "tomb raid," which was aired on the Discovery Channel in early 2007. It was an intriguing performance, as is the book, The Lost Tomb of Jesus, by Simcha Jacobovici and Charles R. Pellegrini. French scholar Andre LeMaire and Professor James Tabor from the University of North Carolina in Charlotte gave academic and archeological credence to the claim that in the Talpiot Cave ten ossuaries were discovered, six of which born the names of Jesus, Son of Joseph; Mary; Joses (brother of Jesus); and Mariamene e Mara (Mary Magdalene); Yehuda bar Jeshua ("son of Jesus"); and one labeled Matthew, perhaps another relative.

It is not our purpose to debate the merit of their claim. I tend to agree with those who warn that the excitement of a few scholars and filmmakers has caused a rush to a faulty conclusion. There have been more than enough scholars, preachers and lay persons who have jumped to the defense of the Biblical story of the resurrection and ascension. Tabor reassured the Church that if this discovery is proven true, it need not cast doubt on the Biblical accounts of the resurrection of Jesus; all it would mean was that the resurrection was more of a spiritual power than a physical body coming back from the grave.

Based on the New Testaments texts, it has always been a revered article of Christian faith that if Jesus returned from death in a physical body, i.e., not a deified or spiritual body, then the body which ascended into heaven must also be a physical, mortal, human body. The problem for some is that if you gaze at this possibility too long, it begins to stare back. The Ascension of our Lord is as difficult to incorporate into a modern frame of mind as is the Resurrection itself. But if the risen physical body did not go into the sky, where did it go? It must be somewhere here on earth.

For our purposes, let us accept that the traditional view point is amenable to most Christians. And let us assume that the findings in the Talpiot Cave do not include the body (or more accurately, the bones of the body) of Jesus of Nazareth. What the new speculations primarily mean to those who teach and preach the Gospel is that some flexibility regarding what might have happened to the body of Jesus is necessary, unless we chose to ignore the possibility of new discoveries. The precise location of the body of Jesus has always been a mystery. It is surely possible for a Creator who made the universe to lift a physical human body up to the heavens, but some find it unlikely that such a feat would be required.

INTRODUCTION

With each new dawn, a little of Easter morning is waiting to come into our lives. Whether it peeks out of the deep cold of winter, flashes by in the changing colors of autumn, lazies around in the too-hot summer or sprouts forth in the bright, refreshing spring, we need to rise to greet it and to capture it. We need to be absorbed into the Resurrection moment, not only on Easter Sunday, but on all our days in all our decades on earth. I bring these "responses to the Resurrection" to you in hopes that wherever you are on the merry-go-round of human existence, you will feel lifted up and drawn to a broader vision of what it means to feel the surge of newness in this life and the next. The Resurrection (with a capital R) refers to the moment when Jesus the Christ was raised from the tomb. A resurrection can happen almost any time you need it. I hope this book will help to deepen your faith and allow you to borrow on the power and peace of the Resurrected Jesus with gusto and grace.

Most of the following chapters began as sermons preached along the way. I have chosen not to update them nor explain them in their settings. I also chose not to identify when the sermons were preached. A few go back to my first ecclesiastical assignment (1961-1966) at the Shadyside Presbyterian Church in Pittsburgh. I left my college chaplaincy at Carnegie-Mellon University to become an assistant pastor at that great, historic congregation. There, my eyes were opened to the glories of the Gospel. It was at Shadyside I discovered that ministry matters, that sermons and prayers and good cheer can change peoples' lives. This conviction has, thankfully, never left me. Pastors often chatter on about the ups and downs of ministry, about how some assignments are filled with troubles and woe. But I am as excited, grateful and satisfied to be a minister of the Gospel now at age 70 as I was back when I was a bright and shiny 25 years old.

The widely read Barbara Brown Taylor recently published a book she called Leaving Church. It annoyed me. It seems as though she got fed up wearing her clerical collar everywhere she went. She writes that it sort of choked the Church right out of her. Seems to me it would have been easier to remove the collar and pass herself off as a normal person. Or she could have applied for transfer into Presbyterianism, where most ministers choose not to harness themselves to a collar. But Taylor jumped ship (or Church) and swam (or sallied) up the road of uncertainty to become a professor at a small college in Georgia.

I admit that once in a while I have cast my longing eyes over the fence into the waving fields of teaching. It sure looks easier having summers off, along with Christmas and Easter weeks, and all the ordinary weekends thrown in, too, plus a long sabbatical now and then to catch up. And of course, anyone in his or her right mind would not choose to live in downtown Atlanta when the grassy knolls and quiet streets await in a small college town in Georgia. There, you can think or nap all day long and face an entirely new congregation every four years. Anyone, that is, except those of us who feel called to ministry. No thanks—her lifestyle is not for me.

Seems I remember our Lord likened the ministerial calling to hanging a yoke around the neck, which does not sound all that comfortable to begin with. No one ever promised a quiet country garden. "Until they do to you what they did to Jesus, you have no reason to complain," my buddy Festus used to say. When Peggy and I were off to a parish assignment 1,300 miles away from our beloved families and friends in Pittsburgh, my father added, "Quit shuffling around about it, Rich. If you are going, go! No man, having put his hand to the plow and looking back, is fit for the kingdom of God!'" No need to cast a sullied view towards anyone who decides to get up and go, but knowing all they know about ministry and the kingdom of God on earth, I still choose to hang tight, dig in, fulfill my promise and keep on trying to change the world for good.

A couple of these chapters originated during the three short years we served in Parkwood Presbyterian Church, north of Pittsburgh. After we returned from the Ph.D. chase at St. Mary's College at the University of St. Andrews in Scotland in the late 1960s, we were called to a congregation that had resulted from the merger of two churches a few years earlier. Of course, residue of conflict still lingered. But the new church building was situated on 10 rolling acres in a thriving American suburb. All we had to do was open the doors and watch the people stream in. It was really not that easy, but in those years (1969-1972) in Allison Park, I found some new approaches to preaching and pastoring. I discovered that the harder you work on a sermon throughout the week, the better it is likely to be on Sunday morning. The Parkwood people were good to us, even if some of them felt we were always looking up over the horizon to our next charge.

Some chapters originated at the Southminister Presbyterian Church in Mt. Lebanon, Pennsylvania. If you read closely, you will see how they bear that imprint. When I arrived at Southminster in 1972 as a young senior pastor, I was captivated by the multi-tasking required in a large church with more than 30 employees on staff. The mid-1970s were peculiar years. Although the intense conflicts and protests for Civil Rights in the 1960s had become less intense, the search for compatibility and communication between the races and sexes were in full swing, as they still are. The pathway to the pulpit took me through the lives, joys and worries of those days. I am still amazed at the breadth of expectations a congregation brings to worship.

I never toot the family horn about how well we did this or that, but the good folk at Southminster, who shared the quest to be the Church of the Living Christ, and who supported and loved Peggy and me and our children, can take a deep bow for what was accomplished in those dozen years. It was at Southminster that the opening edition of this volume was first published and where Desert Ministries, Inc., began. We will be forever grateful for those who helped us get it started. A precious lot of what I know was gifted to me on Washington Road by people who remain as dear to us as anyone else on earth.

When God called us to the First Presbyterian Church of Ft. Lauderdale, Florida, in the summer of 1983, most people told me that my main task would be to master the ways of a congregation that more than doubled with part-time residents and tourists during the winter season. Summers would be easy, they said. The reigning problem of the day was the surfeit of rowdy Spring-break college students, who descended on the southeast coast of Florida and tore our town to pieces every year. "Where the Boys Are," a popular motion picture of the day, tells all about it. But the college breakers were soon edged out, the oceanfront became a mini-Riviera and the winter residents came to comprise less than one-third of our congregation. Peggy and I arrived just as Ft. Lauderdale was coming out of the ground, quite literally. It soon became the large, year-round thriving city that it is today.

August Burghard, the noted author, who unfortunately was near the end of his life when I accepted the call to come to his church, caught on instantly. After I described my goals during my first visit, he said, "The time is right for you, Dr. Cromie. We need a big city boy to take us through the changes that are coming down here."

The change-weary membership of the old town, as well as the winter visitors, were soon surpassed in numbers and ambitions by the burgeoning influx of new, young, dynamic families in industry, manufacturing, culture and healthcare, along with those who majored in professional sports, building towering condos along the water, and all the rest. I have often felt it must have been similar to being an ordained minister in New York City in the 1850s.

Those three "congregations" in one, and the whirl of the newness around us, required us to scramble and shuffle as we mixed and matched the Church staff, programs and weekly sermons into a suitable compromise, remembering the variety of needs of God's children. I found that almost no one knew how to plan and carry out this unique specialized ministry in a vacation land.

Times of rapid change bring their own demands. I still think of the little lady who was lamenting the myriad of changes that perplexed most old time residents of the once-quiet vacation town. I told her that in the time and providence of God, it all meant that progress was coming, and we would all have to get used to it. "Oh," she said, "I'm in favor of progress. It's all these changes I can't stand!"

For most of the last decade of my active ministry, I served as preaching pastor at The Royal Poinciana Chapel in Palm Beach, Florida. The town of Palm Beach is an American treasure and a unique place to preach. The Chapel had the resources to do almost anything it chose. The island city is enormously wealthy, but it too, was in transition. Not too many years had passed since Royal Poinciana had been a summer chapel that opened around Thanksgiving and literally closed its doors sometime after Easter. No pledge campaign was necessary, or would have been tolerated. I promised never to preach a stewardship sermon for as long as I was there. (No one had to twist my arm to solidify the promise.) Through its century of service as a preaching station for winter visitors, three yearly offerings brought more than enough money: Easter, Thanksgiving and Christmas. There were almost no youth programs, only one Bible study, a couple adult education events and a yearly boutique-bazaar that served as the sole source of revenue for benevolences. In time, the Chapel added increased funds for benevolences and also an expanding scholarship programs for minorities and members and friends of the Chapel. Summer attendance grew. I am happy to write that my successor at the Chapel continues to move it forward with all his might.

I learned a lot there about ministering to a vacation-minded congregation, whose primary interests were their churches back home. Mixing in the growing younger population on the island with needs of its own throughout the year, I also re-learned a lesson from Shadyside: that people's needs remain the same, no matter how much money or power or pressures they have. They still want to be reassured that they matter to Christ, and that in his Resurrection, the ultimate issue of life and death is solved. Each and every one of us needs God's love and peace.

Our central theme in this volume is how we can understand and announce the Resurrection of Jesus Christ to the present mind and milieu. Now and then you will note some exegetical analysis of where the Gospel records came from and what they mean today. At times I admit that some lingering questions are not answered here. In my opinion, there are some concerns about the New Testament stories of the death and resurrection of Jesus which might never be answered. Perhaps they will someday: we are promised in the Bible that what is hidden will one day be made known. Meanwhile, the message bears repeating and should be applied to the living of our days on earth. I am certain that the purpose of the incarnation was not and is not to allow those of us who call ourselves Christians to have an easy route to heaven through the resurrected Jesus. Christ came to bring us abundant life here on earth, here and now. Eternal life is not the purpose of the Gospel—that is in the hands of God anyway. If we are raised with Christ, then we should raise ourselves up to help those who are forced to live in the spiritual, emotional and other difficult "deserts" of the earth.

So whatever "season" you are in just now, I ask you to allow St. Paul and the writers of the Gospels to sit down beside you as you read this book. Let them take you by the hand and work themselves into your soul. Then as you rise, find the newness that God has planned for you alone and take it with you into the city streets and all the troubled places on the earth.

The original Resurrection came as a great surprise. No one expected it; no one was waiting for it. No one. The public vendors, priests and people were sleeping off the rigors of Holy Week. Even our Lord's closest friends and followers went to bed that Saturday night with nothing more than a weak wish, a pale yearning that his death on Good Friday would not be the end of the story. In times of grief we all look for something to transcend the hour of death. The Bible records that no one anticipated that he would come back to life. To be sure, Jesus had predicted that he would, but if they had heard him, they forgot as the weekend rolled around. I mean, dead men do not rise—they tell no tales, right? Wrong—in this case, anyway. Resurrection is not within the range of normalcy, but if you are alive and awake to the resurrection moment when it comes, you had better hold it and keep it and love it for all your days.

Back at the beginning, the believers knew that it had occurred and considered it a good reminder that we must be available to God's surprises and keep looking around corners to make sure we do not miss them. As St. Paul finally concluded, "If Christ has not been raised, our faith is futile, and all who have fallen asleep in Christ have perished. If for this life only we have hoped in Christ, we are of all people most to be pitied" (I Corinthians 15: 19).

Today, 2000 years later, I can testify that I have seen the Lord. I have experienced the presence, power and peace of the Risen One who came to expand our lives here, and to give us eternal life for all time to come. I want to share my joy with you.

In some ways, my approach to the Resurrection and its aftermath has broadened over the years. In another way, it seems to have stayed the same. When I re-read the various drafts of this revised edition, I became aware that I seem to be trying to convince myself that the Easter story is true. As I declare my belief in the resurrected Jesus Christ, I find myself producing arguments against it. I seldom rest my case in what the Bible's English translation seems to say. I need to look at both sides before I decide. But I have been conscious that some are not persuaded by repetitions of the same old story—or they need to hear it from a new vantage point.

Perhaps it comes out of my debate experience at Pitt. We won most national tournaments in which we competed, thanks to careful preparation and research plus rigorous cross examination in our bi-weekly practices. Bob Patton, a DMI Board Member who also debated in college, came up to me one Sunday in Pittsburgh after services and chuckled. "Well, that was a good First Affirmative," meaning that while my sermon was acceptable, it was time for a good First Negative. That is the way formal college debate proceeds. A convincing argument is set forth and it prompts a good First Negative response, which exposes its weaknesses. Then the Second Affirmative responds, as does the Second Negative. I keep thinking that some learned debating coach like Rocky Newman at Pitt or

Mel Moorhouse at Westminster College in New Wilmington PA. might be sitting in the pews and will rise up to critique my sermon when I have finished.

Someone at Parkwood Church told me that I should speak with more authority and tell the parishioners what they should believe. I was sorry to disappoint him; but I have never felt it my responsibility to tell other Christians what to believe. Many preachers do, as if they had secrets whispered in their ears alone. I am always a little leery of pounding my truth into the heads of others. I think it is my job to make them think and work out their own conclusions. Spoon-feeding the little Christians I leave to someone else.

I am not apologizing. Far from it! I think the Lord God is pleased when we search for his truth. I think sometimes "maybe" is enough. "My ways are not your ways; neither my thoughts your thoughts." Some clergy parrot back their opinion taken from a drive-by look at the Bible or what someone else has told them. They feel this makes them the final authority on everything. The Bible says, "Test everything, but hold fast to what is good." I have tried to do both with integrity and conviction. I hope it is evident in these responses to the Resurrection. I welcome you to examine the fruits of my labors.

I

BREAKFAST BY THE GALILEAN SEA

Text from John 21

I want to warn you at the start— caution you, anyway — that you have to watch out for old John, the author of the fourth Gospel. He likes happy endings, he likes to keep it simple, and he likes to tie up loose ends. He was a fine Christian gentleman, a devoted follower of Jesus, one who earned the title of "The Beloved Disciple." We know much about what Jesus said and did due to the fourth Gospel. You can trust John with the truth, but you have to watch out for his personalized approach to the life of Jesus.

As I said, John was fond of tying up loose ends and offering happy endings. As an example, after Thomas said that he doubted Jesus had risen from the dead, John is the only Gospel writer who tells us that Christ came back and spoke to Thomas. Thomas said, "My Lord and my God." That put Thomas back on the first team.

John is also the only one of the four Gospel writers who tells us about the death and resurrection of Lazarus. It is remarkable that Matthew, Mark and Luke never even mentioned something so grandly miraculous. I don't know why. But John wanted us to know that Jesus loved his friend Lazarus, who was Mary and Martha's brother, and that he wept at his tomb just before he brought him back to life. John is also the only one who tells us about the miracle at the wedding feast in Galilee, when Jesus turned the water into wine. He wanted us to know that our Lord and his disciples were friendly people who loved family and friends and enjoyed life and weddings.

Conversely, John never tells us that Jesus rejected his mother and brothers when they came to visit him one day when he was busy. The synoptic writers tell it (Luke 8:19-21 and Matthew 12:46-50). He probably knew about it, but he did not include it. Apparently, he did not like that kind of story. He does not tell us that Jesus was rejected by his own family and friends in Nazareth. (Luke 4:20-30 and Mark 6:1-6), nor does he include the beheading of Jesus' cousin, John the Baptist, by Herod in appreciation of his stepdaughter's fancy dancing.

So when we come to this last chapter in his Gospel, we should not be surprised that John alone tells the captivating story of how Simon Peter was restored to leadership by Jesus. In the other three Gospels, Peter is left having disgraced himself by the betrayal of his Lord the night before the crucifixion, but John likes to keep the good guys looking good.

This could be what happens when you reach a ripe old age: you come to worry less about details and sad things, and lean more on the simple truths of the Gospel. The great theologian Karl Barth said that as he grew older and was nearing the end, he was asked about the most important and essential thing he knew. He replied quietly, "Jesus loves me, this I know, for the Bible tells me so. Little ones to him belong. We are weak, but he is strong." Can you believe it? How grandly simple! In the end, it is child-like acceptance and surrender that matter most.

Remember: John wrote his book some 60, or maybe even 70, years after the death and resurrection of Jesus. That is a long time, time to set aside the nonessentials, time to bring it down to the one or two thoughts you cannot live without. Unamuno, the revered Spanish existentialist, told his students, "Worry not about what others think; worry only over what God thinks of you!" he said. It takes many of us a long time to learn that.

Anyway, I love the way John tells the story of breakfast by the Galilean Sea. The disciples are out on the water fishing when a man appears on the shore. The man was Jesus, but they did not know it. Why? In some of the post-Resurrection appearances, people did not recognize Jesus when he first appeared. This happened to Mary Magdalene on Easter morning in the Garden and to Cleopas and his friend on the road to Emmaus. Jesus walked beside them, and they did not know who he was.

But here at the seaside breakfast, the reason was simple: they did not know it was Jesus because it was early morning, the mist was still on the lake and the man on the shore was too far away to see clearly. There is nothing mysterious or other-worldly about that. This is not a spiritual body trying to break back into human form. It is the real, live, walking, talking Jesus. A couple minutes later, when he invited them to have breakfast, they would be certain who it was. After all, you do not sit down and eat and drink with a ghost, now do you?

To get the larger picture, we need to go back for a minute to the beginning of Chapter 21. After the crushing disappointment of the crucifixion, some of the disciples left Jerusalem and went back to Galilee. It says Jesus told them to go there and said he would come and meet them. But I have never thought that was why they journeyed home. Nah. Even though Mary Magdalene had seen him outside the tomb, and there were hints that he had appeared in some form or another, I think they were bewildered and decided to go back to the little town from which they had come to clear their minds.

They were most likely in Bethsaida. John says they were on the Sea of Tiberius, but Tiberius is the name John uses for what the others call the Galilean Sea. Tiberius was the largest and most influential city on the Lake. Notice that just seven of them were there. I am not sure where the other four were. Judas was gone, of course; he hanged himself. Peter, James and John were there. The two unnamed disciples were surely Andrew and Philip. Thomas the twin was there, along with Nathaniel of Cana. It would have been a long and perilous journey on foot for the 75 miles from Jerusalem to Tiberius. It was an almost identical journey, by the way, to the one Joseph and Mary had taken 34 years earlier down to Bethlehem, she being great with child. Travel conditions would have been dreadful off the system of Roman roads that ran up and down the country. It would have taken them a long while to get there, possibly seven or eight days and nights. And immersed in their bewilderment and grief, now that their guide and master was gone, it would have seemed all the longer: the road home from the funeral of someone you love is the longest road in all the world.

So, let's assume it was a week or so after Easter by the time they got home. I imagine it was worse when they arrived, although the Scripture does not mention it. Knowing something of human nature, I can easily guess the ridicule the disciples faced from their friends and families. "Hey, lookee here, the great adventurers have returned. Look at 'em. The boys are back home again, dragging their tails behind them, Hey Abe, Simon is back — heard he changed his name to Peter; and there's his stupid little brother. And the Sons of Zebbie who left their father and the family business are back again. Hey Salome, the Jesus freaks are back home and broke! I told them it would come to nothing. Hey Pete, if you ever need a job, come and see me. Maybe you can till the fields or sweep the streets or mend somebody's nets."

Distasteful business it is eating crow, having to admit that you were as dumb as the younger brother who ran off and wasted his inheritance. Only his father threw a party when he came back, but nobody whipped a party up for the broken disciples. They had believed in their neighbor, Jesus. They had bet their lives that Jesus the carpenter's son would prove to be the One. They hoped to find a happy ending. But by God, it did not look that way the afternoon they came shuffling home, empty-handed and empty-hearted. The weight of carrying an emotional burden is one of the heaviest of all. And the condemnations that matter most are those ones we make on ourselves. You can be sure they were down on themselves and feeling stupid.

But I learned a long time ago—and maybe you did too—that the worst mistake of all is not taking a risk in the first place. You seldom look foolish staying home and playing it close to the vest. A recluse seldom makes a fool of himself chasing after the hucksters or the helpers of the world. Those who play it safe never have to crawl back and beg forgiveness from their families. The safe church which never takes a risk never gets into trouble. "Those who are down need fear no fall," the shepherd boy sings in Bunyan's _Pilgrims Progress_.

For every risk, there is a corresponding loss. Old Zebediah, Judah, Elizabeth and every Tom, Dick and Harry in town must have looked pretty good that day when Peter, Andrew, James, John and Phillip came dragging home with Nathanial and Thomas following behind. What to do next was the problem.

So, it is little wonder that volatile Simon Peter, whose heights were higher and depths were deeper than the rest, decided he was going to do something rather than sit around and ponder all the could-have-beens. Some people are that way. I call it the "Simon of Cyrene" complex, after the man who was forced to carry the cross. At least he had something to carry. All the others could do on the Via Dolorosa was watch and weep. When you are down on your luck or depressed, get up and do something. It's good therapy.

Simon Peter knew that. He said, "I don't know about the rest of you, but I am going fishing."

Good choice, Simon. He was a fisherman by trade; he was born to the sea, bred to follow the path of any one of the 22 species that traversed the Jordan River Valley, dependent on it for his life and livelihood.

The tense of the Greek verb John uses here — _hupago_— and his sentence structure could allow us to believe that Simon Peter meant to have more than a momentary respite from his faltering patience and oppressive gloom. He could have meant to say, "It was three good years, but it's over. Finito. Over and out!" Once a fisherman, always a fisherman and down on himself, he could have thought, "I am going back to my former life, fully determined never to allow my dreams to run away with me again. Now I'm going fishing." The world does not reward

6

you for great adventures, unless you succeed. The ones who worship risk-taking are the ones who win, but oh dear, they often lose as well.

The six of them understood and said "We'll go, too." Nathanial wasn't even a fisherman, by the way, but he went along. Once they were out on the sea, they sailed all night long, but caught nothing. Doggone it all: they couldn't even pull a little break with all they had been through.

But just as day was breaking through the morning mists along the Sea of Galilee, they saw a man on the shore, or rather heard him. His voice called out to them in a Greek idiom that translates something like, "Children, have you any fish?" or "Friends, have you caught anything?" *(May ti prosthagion exete?)* When they said no, he said, "Then, cast your net on the other side of the boat, and you will find some."

This has always puzzled me. I could never figure out how a Nazarean carpenter, even if he were the Son of God incarnate, would know more about how to fish the Galilean Sea than those four fishermen. No disrespect intended for our Lord. But then I read what Professor William Barclay wrote in his commentary on John. He said that it is not uncommon, due to the way the morning light strikes the water, for a man to stand on the shore and direct those in the boat. He can see what they are missing. It takes the miracle out of the story, but eliminates the jurisdictional dispute.

Either way, it says they followed his advice, and when they cast their net from the right-hand side of the boat, 153 good-sized fish were trapped in the net. That made it so heavy, they could hardly haul it in.

It was just about the time they were counting the fish, or just plain reveling in their good fortune, that John finally recognized the man on shore. "Oh, glory be, Peter, look! It's him! It's the Lord! It's Jesus!" As far as they knew, Jesus was in Heaven, but there he was, standing on the shore.

Simon Peter, being the rambunctious one, sprang into the sea. He was better at responding to a good idea than at creating one. He must have looked foolish early that morning. But twenty-nine years later Peter would look far more foolish and stupid than he ever did that morning when he leapt, splashed, gulped and snorted his way to the shore, where the Lord was waiting. By 62 A.D. he would be hanging upside down on a cross on one of Rome's seven hills, dying that way because he said he was not worthy to be crucified right side up, as Jesus had been, looking beaten and forsaken until he would arrive on that unnamed shore we obligingly call "the other side," where Christ was waiting. He will be there when your days and mine are through. The dreamer dies, but not the dream.

When Peter got out on land, he saw a charcoal fire with fish cooking and bread warming alongside it right there by sea. Jesus said, "Bring me some of the fish you have caught," and they did. "Come and have breakfast with me," Jesus said, and they did that, too.

Now, there is a little problem here. I suppose this is as good a time as any to tell you that there is a lot of controversy among Biblical scholars surrounding this story in John 21. Many cannot believe it actually happened as the Gospel says it did. Hardly anyone who is serious about John believes that this story (John 21) is an original part of the Gospel. For one thing, John 20 says that Peter had already seen the Lord in Jerusalem.

A couple of days later, it seems unlikely that he would not recognize him. It could be the story of a first post-Resurrection encounter that was tacked on to John, say 70 years after the death of Christ.

The Gospel of John is a complete unit without it, ending naturally with the Resurrection and the appearance to Thomas and the others. To say that the story was added does not attack its verity, or the details of the breakfast by the Galilean Sea. My view is that John himself added it later. But some think this episode may be an allegory, whose purpose might have been to reinstate Peter as the leader of the Apostles. After all, he had fallen into disgrace around another charcoal fire, where the cock crowed at dawn after he had betrayed his Lord three times.

Without this story, the Gospel ends with Peter disgraced. So when he later becomes a prominent leader and the Bishop of Rome, such an ending would have seemed incongruous. John writes a happy ending for Peter, in which Jesus charges him to go and tend his sheep. Remember, I warned you that John likes happy endings.

So now, note the lovely touch John puts on the ending, as he remembers the conversation around the fire that morning. No one dared to ask who Jesus was, where he had been or what it was like to be dead. (Many times I have wished they would have asked him). In the latter part of John 21, Jesus asks Peter if he really loves Him. Peter replies "Yes," three times (to match the denials, I guess), "you know that I love you." Christ charges him to tend his sheep, to feed his lambs, to tend his sheep again—that is, to carry on his work of ministering to the sick and dying, the aged, the homeless, widows and orphans in Galilee, in all Judea and in the world beyond.

The world can be a lonely place, even when you are in the

middle of a crowd. In the city streets with the hungry and unemployed, out in the mission field fraught with dangers untold, in Nazareth or Jerusalem then or now, in Tel Aviv or Beruit or Gaza today, down the road in Jericho, on the banks of the ancient Jordan River, in the ghettos, across the tracks, and all along the banks of the Tigris and Euphrates or any other sea or river, the world can get you down. What we should do about it is our next assignment.

I invite you to sit down to a quiet little chit-chat with our Risen Lord sometime after Easter, and watch him as he walks around the charcoal fire then, or around our private quarters now, serving us one by one. How nice to be in the presence of the Risen Lord! But as you watch his glorious presence, watch out for his command. You are welcome at the breakfast tent, but if you love me, show me by giving of your means and your time and your prayers and your energies to serve the least of my brethren.

"Enjoy the morning, but do not boast or revel in my resur-rected glory. Its purpose was not and is not to impress you as much as to inspire you. Get up, go out and work like fools for my sake. You can live on love. . . love received, love shared and love redeemed."

And you know, by golly, the Disciples did it. They carried on. And you and I can, too. Slave away all night long without success, or since tragedy visited last month, or since you lost your job, or your failing health snuffed out your hope, or your son, or your school, or your bad luck let you down. Slave away while you are still far out to sea. But now and again, look up and over to the beach. You might not know who it is, but from the shores of Galilee, you will hear a voice calling out, "Are you having any luck?" When you hear it, be honest about your needs and do what he says. Tell him you need his help by saying, "Oh Lord, I cannot make it any farther by myself. Tell me what I need to do, and help me do it."

Then spring right into the water and thrash your way to shore. When you finally arrive, he will be there waiting; the fire will still be warm, and breakfast will be ready. He will serve you and give you what you need, just as he did in John 21. After he had served them breakfast, he sent them off to save the world. Whatever else occurred—even another crucifixion and agonizing death—with just the memory of his words, they lived happily ever after. And so shall you and I, for now and evermore, Amen.

II

THE FIRST EASTER SERMON

"Mary Magdalene went and said to the Disciples,
'I have seen the Lord.'"

JOHN 20:18

Had it not been for that first Easter morning, the world would be a poorer place indeed. It is difficult to sort through the details of exactly what happened from reading the New Testament. Many have tried to find some kind of harmony in the various resurrection texts, but it is a stretch to try to edit it down to a consistent story. The four Gospel writers sing the same lovely song. But if you think of them as a Barbershop Quartet in which each one sings a different note, you will hear it all more clearly. Matthew, Mark and Luke are in a synoptic key - that is, they are similar - while John has his own unique and individual range.

Look at what the Gospels say happened when Mary Magdalene went up to the sepulcher. Luke says that Joanna went along, with the mother of James joining them. Matthew tells us there were only two: Mary Magdalene and the other Mary. Mark adds Salome to the group. John writes that Mary Magdalene was alone.

Anyway, Mary was carrying some spices for anointing the body of her departed Lord. But when she arrived, Mark and Luke tell us that the huge stone that had been guarding the entrance had been rolled away. It surprised her, of course; and when she looked or walked into the tomb, she found it empty. She was by now befuddled and dismayed: all she wanted to do was spread some precious preservative ointment on her friend, and she couldn't find his body. She thought someone had moved it, or even stolen it. Then she saw an angel sitting on the rolled-away stone, and he told her not to worry or be afraid, for Jesus had risen from the dead and was alive again.

When she went back out of the tomb, she saw a man standing there. It was Jesus, but she did not recognize him for reasons we do not know. She thought it was the gardener. He spoke to her, calling her by name. "Mary…" She looked up and saw him, and then she knew who it was. There was no doubt in her mind that Jesus was standing there. It was no ghost, no apparition, no ephemeral vision and no projection on her retina. It was The Lord.

She was so excited that she ran back to the disciples and delivered the first Easter sermon: the preacher was Mary; the congregation was the disciples and some others. The place was most likely an upper room in Jerusalem where the 11 Disciples (Judas had hanged himself; maybe 10, for it is not certain that Thomas was there.) and the others had crowded themselves in. The sermon was delightfully short: "I have seen the Lord!" she said.

I. The first thing to notice is that Mary Magdalene was preaching about something she knew first hand: "I" have seen him. It was not a rumor she picked up in the streets of Jerusalem. No one had heard the angel or seen the Risen

Christ over by the graveyard. She saw him, and heard him. She was an eyewitness. You cannot speak with authority about such a stupendous occurrence unless you have experienced it or until you have seen it. Mary was relaying what she knew.

Throughout the centuries, all doubts and arguments about the truthfulness of her words cannot change the power of her simple declaration: "I saw him." The Russian author Alexander Solzhenitsyn once wrote that a simple truth is more powerful than all the armies in the world. He discovered that himself in Stalin's Gulag concentration camps.

Now, you might want to quibble with what she said. Do so if you like. Some say that Mary Magdalene was biased, or that her grief overpowered her and she projected the presence of her Master. Others have said that the words were put into her mouth at a later date by some unknown compiler of the stories of Jesus, who was fabricating the Resurrection for future use. Some of the early Gnostic Gospel writers removed Mary from the story completely. They said that the Son of God would never have appeared to a woman. Other critics have pointed to the myriad of other ancient religions whose records also tell of a resurrected hero who came back from the dead (see The Uses of the Past by Herman J. Mueller).

Quibble if you must. But remember that you are up against someone who was there. She saw Jesus with her own eyes. The Bible does not try to prove that she was right; it just accepts it. St. Paul attempts some evidence later on to make his readers think about it, but he also rests his case with those who saw the risen Lord. He included his vision on the road to Damascus as a proof-positive eyewitness account. You might have your own private litmus test that you use to distinguish truth from falsehood. Trot it out now and apply it to the task. Mine usually rests its case in the testimony of those I know and trust. I warn you: Mary is a friend of mine.

We will come back to the various proofs of the Gospel records later in this book. Just let me say here that there are many ways of seeing. Some see within their souls; some see without their eyes. Anyone can come to see that which has been there all the time. Some see with their eyes, but Jesus warned that some who see still do not see. Eyewitnesses often differ in their recollections of what happened. I have had that experience several times myself.

But not Mary. She had just rushed back from the tomb to say that the stone had been rolled away and the garden grave was empty. Something had happened to the body. She admitted that she was puzzled, but then she saw him. What's more, he spoke to her. She relied on the evidence of her own eyes and ears and soul. "I have seen the Lord!" Maybe she missed something, but it appears she did not.

In his novel, A Mass for the Dead, William Gibson wrote about the day he was tidying up his parents' house after they had passed away. He picked up his mother's gold-rimmed spectacles to read her favorite Bible. He sat down in her comfy chair by the window, placed her tiny spectacles on his nose and tried to see what she saw in the Scripture. He reached out for some slender thread of her faith, once so alive and vibrant in her. It didn't work. Perhaps he was too preoccupied with the empty household, or with his grief, or with trying to figure it all out, but he could not recapture anything. He said he felt as silly as he must have looked wearing her little glasses. His mother's faith could not be borrowed. Another's faith can be an impetus for your own, but like a fragile summer plant, it cannot be transplanted. We can admire and envy it, but we can never possess it, unless it becomes our own. Another's faith can be a good example, but each of us must walk that lonesome, individual valley by ourselves. It is not faith until it is your faith.

Neither can you borrow it from Mary Magdalene. "I have seen the Lord" worked for her, maybe because she strolled up to the empty tomb herself, walked in and came out to see the Lord. That could be the key to seeing the living Jesus—coming back out of the tomb and seeing him yourself. Until YOU see it, the truth belongs to someone else.

II. Now shift the emphasis a little to make the sentence read, "I have <u>seen</u> the Lord." Father Teilhard de Chardin, the French paleontologist and theologian, in the midst of all his heavy work, caught the gist of it when he wrote about what it means "to see." "We might say that the whole of life lies in that one verb. To see or to perish, is the very condition laid upon everything which makes up the universe," he writes in <u>The Phenomenon of Man.</u> I agree: our eyes have seen the coming of a lot of things, but we can miss them, too.

It was true in the rugged jungle, when those early creatures had to be able to see to escape from natural predators. It was true with Abraham and Sarah, who through the eyes of faith saw on down through the valley where God commanded them to go. It was true at the time of the Exodus, when the Jewish people had to see through the Desert of Sinai to the time when their 40-year trek would end, and they could finally claim the Promised Land. It was also true when they endured their captivity in Babylon. Their eyes were focused on the route back home, which God had promised. "If I forget you, O Jerusalem, let my right hand wither! Let my tongue cleave to the roof of my mouth." (Psalm 137:5) Sometimes all you have are the eyes of memory.

It was difficult to see God clearly when they were beaten and captured by successive powers who kept marching across the Fertile Crescent. It was hard to see the good when old King Herod decided to slaughter all their male children under the age of two. And it was most difficult to see how something good could arise from a dreadful crucifixion and tragedy, when the curtain of the Temple was torn in two and graves exploded open all over the city.

And on that first Easter morning, Mary Magdalene had to see beyond the moment. "It is not what you look at; it's what you see," Thoreau once wrote. Seeing is what matters, believing follows on the heels of what you see. What I see is what I end up believing is there.

"Only that day dawns to which we are awake." (Thoreau) The only daybreak we see is the one we are up and prepared for. If you get so wound up in the events of the workaday world, or in the petty complaints that things are not done the way you want them, or if you try to keep within the boundaries of what you can define and describe and master on your own, you will miss it.

The morning looked sad and tragic to Mary Magdalene, and maybe to the other Mary and Salome and Joanna, as they came up to the sepulcher. The lonely little group was groping its way along, laden with funereal spices, sometime before the dawn when it was still too dark to see what was going on. Luke says their heads were bowed down. Maybe that is why they did not see him at first. You have to look up before your eyes can see who is there.

But he was there, standing beside them with the living message that all was well again. Dead men do not rise; but

18

there he was, alive and well, and they almost missed him. So wound up were they in what was going on in the corners of their own minds, so afraid and troubled, so angry and bewildered, their eyes so filled with tears that they did not allow themselves to see him—not at first, anyway.

In time he made himself known to them. Then they believed. His living message brought the news they needed. After that, they could face anything, just as he had. The ultimate enemy called death had been defeated. Victory was at hand. If that is not true, then this life is a hoax and the cynics win the day. Jean Paul Sartre would be your existential hero: "Every existing thing is born without reason, prolongs itself by weakness, and dies by chance," he said. To Sartre, human life had no God-given purpose at all. But Sartre and his kin are wrong. Existentialism is as dead as they are. Easter shows us that the living God has conquered. Life does have meaning, and as Robert Browning said, "To find it is our meat and drink." Family strife can never conquer all that is good and wholesome. A debilitating illness, albeit awful, can lead to inner joy. Job frustration can never quite destroy. Marriages can dip and sag. Old age can take its toll. But, then along comes Easter, and the upside down is turned right side up again.

Astrophysicists project that eternal darkness will be the fate of the universe. There will be no light and no one will see anything at all. Einstein knew that a static universe was impossible because gravity would never be powerful enough to hold it together. But what of it? If God made the world for his purpose, then its purpose does not end when it physically deteriorates or is swallowed up by the empty holes of outer space. Into the hollow of time beyond our time and space, Mary

Magdalene's little sermon echoes: "I have seen the Lord!" And nothing else will ever matter.

III. Third and last, make her statement to read: "I have seen the <u>Lord</u>!" It is a matter of emphasis. The Gospel story is clear about who and what she saw: it was not an image; it was not a projection of her bewildered psyche; it was not an imprint for a life-less hope. It was Jesus. When she saw the Lord, she was no longer at the eternal mercy of Rome or Herod. Life does not count its paces at the whim and accident of time. In the aftermath of Easter, the third day always comes. In the words of Tennyson:

> Oh yet we trust that somehow good
> Will be the final goal of all. . .
> That nothing walks with aimless feet;
> That not one life shall be destroyed –
> Or cast as rubbish to the void -
> When God hath made the pile complete.
> (<u>In Memoriam</u>)

We are not made to stare into darkness and uncertainty forever. Remember Nietzsche warned that if you stare into an abyss for too long, the abyss will begin to stare back. Then you will be a goner. In your loneliest moments you need to know that something, someone, is there, unbounded by the limitations of time and space, untouched by the unpredictable whim of chance. The soldiers tossed the dice on Good Friday afternoon, but the Lord God Almighty did not join them.

We need to know that however long we live, the angels of God's mercy will still be sitting on the huge stone that blocks the way. They will keep watch, and when the moment has arrived, they will roll the stone away. Christ can turn your life around. The Easter message is a place to start. It is the most important one-line sermon you will ever hear: "I have seen the Lord."

I had a professor of Analytic Philosophy in college. He opened his introductory course by storming into the lecture hall and throwing a Bible across the room into the corner. Then he went over, picked it up and threw it down again. "Does this offend anyone?" he asked arrogantly. "I want you to know that we do not tolerate worship of the Bible around here. By enrolling in my course you agree to be grown-ups. In my class you will not lean on the accumulated folklore of your Grandmother's faith. You will use your brains."

It was daunting, especially because he was the one who would fill out the grade book. But I raised my hand anyway and said, "What you do does not offend me, Sir, as you might think. It is, however, a careless way to treat a book that is precious to me." My objection had nothing to do with religion. I thought a man who would throw the Bible across the room would be likely to throw anything else away, too.

I have always felt it was more than coincidence that the same professor threw himself out a seventh story window to his death a few years later. Poor man; he could never live up to a life that had no meaning. And he could never measure up to a life lived on its own. He never rejoiced with Isaiah who saw the Lord in His Temple, high and lifted up. That was my professor's choice, of course, but not a good one in the end.

Each of us needs two focal points: a home and a horizon. We need a place to hang our hat, rest our weary bones, and get our fill of food and sleep. But we also need a horizon, a beckoning vision, a goal, a destination, a land of hopes and dreams, something that transcends the exigencies of this mortal vale. William Barclay said in my presence one day in Scotland, that there are two important moments in your life: the moment you are born and the moment you discover why.

In John Masefield's book, <u>The Trial of Jesus</u>, the character of Longinis was patterned after the centurion in command of the soldiers at the foot of the Cross. The Synoptic Gospels tell of a centurion who looked up and said, "Truly this man is the Son of God" (Matthew 27:54). In Masefield's account, Longinus had returned with his troops from Calvary. That evening, he was summoned to Pontius Pilate to give his daily report. When he finished, Pilate's wife begged him to tell her more about the crucifixion and how the prisoner had died. After Longinus told her, she said, "Longinis, do you think he is dead now? Is he dead and gone?" "No, ma'am," he replied. "Then, where is he?" she asked. "Let loose in the world, where neither Roman nor Jew will ever stop his truth," he replied.

I share Mary's sermon one more time: short and simple, pure and strong: "I have seen the Lord!" For now and forever more, Amen.

III

SNOWFALL
ON AN EASTER MORNING

"Therefore, if anyone be in Christ, he is a new creation;
old things are passed away; behold, all things are become new."
II CORINTHIANS 5:17

One Easter Sunday, a freak snowstorm landed in the North Hills of Pittsburgh. When we awakened in the wee hours to make ready for the sunrise service in the park, our sleepy eyes were greeted by the awesome sight of eight inches of the wettest snow imaginable. I was crushed. Not that I am a stranger to the joys of winter, nor unappreciative of the glories of the snow. I thrive on the cold. Yet I believe that an Easter Sunday morning snowfall is a devilish kind of curse.

Any preacher worth his rock salt can recite from memory how unkind the skies have been on the first day of any week. We watch the weather forecasts with as wary an eye as a snow plow driver. While some men chart the movement of the stars or the fortunes of their favorite hockey team, ministers chart attendances at Sunday services, and bad weather is one of the most common excuses for missing worship. We live with the humbling knowledge that the church usually comes in second to a lot of other commitments. If the weather is slightly bad, people say that it is too cold to go out on Sunday morning. If it's a little worse, everyone goes skiing. If it's overly warm, the church will be too hot. If it's just right, golfers play golf and others go away for the weekend.

I once saw a cartoon in which a golfer rushed up to the first tee one Sunday morning and apologized that he was late. "I am sorry to keep you waiting", he murmured. "It was a toss-up between playing golf and going to church. Can you believe it? I had to toss the coin 11 times before the golf course won!" Nor shall I ever forget the seasoned rector chatting with his new assistant as they looked out the study window on a rainy Sunday morning. "Ah", he smiled, "The Lord has delivered the golfers unto us." Well, that snowy Easter Sunday was far worse than a rainy one.

We had planned a joyous sunrise service for the whole community. Then we would have two special indoor worship services with extra-fine music at 9:30 a.m. and 11 a.m. Between and following the Services, lovely receptions were planned for the out-of-town visitors and local guests who were potential new members. It does not take a financial secretary to guess that Easter offerings make up for the dearth of income during the dismal winter months.

But all that was before the snow. Seventeen stalwart worshippers made it to the sunrise service and spent most of the hour shoveling the pathways and steps. Somehow my father made the 15-mile trip to help us shovel snow. Thirty-five or 40 came to the 9:30 service. The Church School classes were nearly empty. Three-fifths of the specially prepared choir didn't show for the 11:00 service, and not one of the invited brass players made it. The remaining two-fifths of the choir sounded more like two fifths than they should have, as they tried to pass off their imbalanced tones as Easter music. I came to the conclusion then that there is a direct relationship between the ability to carry a tune and the aversion to carrying a snow shovel to church. I suppose that in retrospect, we should have been grateful that anyone came at all. It was a bad day at the black rock of the minister's study. And I took the trouble to declare to man and God how unfair it seemed that the Easter holiday was ruined by snow.

But in retrospect, something grand and wonderful happened that morning that moved my psyche. It was probably the Lord's way of chastising me for my irreverence. The reprimand came later that week when I met a friend named Marj Mercer, who directed the Christian education program in a nearby Presbyterian Church. She told me what a grand thing had happened across town at her church, which had also been covered in snow. When she got the children together for their little message, they talked about the snow. One child told of how much fun it was to come to Sunday School on her sled. Another said it looked like God got tired of His dirty old world, so He dropped the snow to make it all bright and new for Easter. "Out of the mouths of babes come wonderful truths." God covers up the darkness of our fears and failures and offers us the pure white snow of a new life in the living Christ.

I cannot improve on that child's delightfully naïve little statement. It gets to the heart of everything we need to know about Easter. Into our hurried, worried world, where we ricochet from one crisis to the next, where the debris accumulates from our broken promises, where we are wedded to the compromises we feel compelled to make, comes the calm and reassuring power and peace of Easter morning.

The Bible treats the first Easter morning as a story, and so should we. It is not meant to be a legal brief at a trial before a judge. It is the record of those who were there, or who heard about it from those who were. The records are not a reasoned argument to prove exactly what happened. If you apply that kind of rigorous examination to it, you will go away without a verdict. It is more like a song or a rhapsody.

One day at Princeton, a student asked Einstein to explain the Theory of Relativity. "Sure, I will be glad to do that for you," he is said to have said. "Come over some afternoon and I will play it for you on my violin." Touché. You have to sing about it first, before you can have command of it in the written word. The spoken word can hardly do the job alone. The Easter thrill is a transcending presence, which belongs more to poetry than to prose. To get it right, allow yourself to get caught up in its majesty, outside of time and space.

There is a Biblical text to greet you too. It comes in Paul's Second Letter to the Corinthians. Chapter 5 begins with mention of the imperishable house we have, one not made with hands, but one eternal in the heavens, gifted to us by the Christ who lived and died and rose again to make us whole. "If anyone be in Christ, he is a new creation; old things are passed away; behold all things are new," Paul declares. Christ can make you new as well, if you pause long enough to allow him to.

SNOWFALL ON AN EASTER MORNING

I. The first idea we need to look at is the news that God can transform his whole world and each of us in it, into something grand and new. That's what Jesus said to Nicodemus, who came to see him. Poor thing — he was a teacher of religion, but he did not have the foggiest notion how to understand the faith he had received. I think he had become weary trying to figure things out with the intellectual tools he had. His proud and successful life was wedded to a host of paltry little things that looked impressive, but were not worth a farthing when it came to finding what he needed deep inside.

Have you ever wondered why Nicodemus came to Jesus? He was a noted Pharisee, a leader of his people. John says he came by night, most likely because he did not want to be seen in the daylight cavorting with this roadside evangelist who claimed he could heal the sick. It was even rumored that Jesus could raise the dead. And the worst impiety of all, Jesus claimed that he was the Messiah, the Son of God on earth. Why do you think Nicodemus went? I think he sneaked out to see Jesus because something was missing from his life, something he had inklings and guesses about, but had never really found. He needed something more. Some little voice inside told him he could find what he needed in the preacher from Nazareth.

He asked questions of the Lord. He told Jesus he came because he had heard great things about him. Jesus was not interested in what he had heard. He abruptly told him that Nicodemus would have to be born again. He would have to start all over again, with a new birth of water and the spirit. "How do I do that? How can I be born again? That would be impossible," the astonished Nicodemus replied. Jesus told him that you need to believe in order to see it. "God so loved the

SOMETIME BEFORE THE DAWN: 27 world that he gave his only son that whoever believes in him shall not perish, but shall have everlasting life." (John 3:16) "And this is the judgment, that light has come into the world, and men loved darkness rather than the light." (3:19) How about it Nicodemus? And you, have you allowed it to happen to you? Your answer to that question is what matters ultimately when you come to Easter morning.

A deep snowfall can ruin Easter Sunday services, but it cannot ruin Easter. It can drop the pure white spirit of the living God over the weak and tawdry movements of the day, just as surely as it fell across the hills of Palestine in ancient times. You can be born again. The old will be covered up, and you will be redirected to the kind of life you need and say you want. That new birth is a gift from the Risen Christ; a whole new life with a whole new attitude will be offered. You do not need to race down an evangelist's aisle weeping; you can also find the newness on your own back porch. It is yours for the asking. Christ has the power to change you. His death and resurrection can cover all your sins, just as snow covers over all the earth.

Snow fell in the Holy Land in Biblical times and still does, up to the depth of a full foot. It can stay in the hills of Palestine all winter long, and it lingers on the heights of Mount Lebanon until the middle of the summer. Snow appears frequently in the Scripture as an emblem of purity: "Though your sins be as scarlet, they shall be whiter than snow". (Isaiah 1:18)

That message has your name written on it. It taps you on the shoulder wherever you are. It tells you that Christ is bringing newness into the middle of any and all the old things you carry inside your inner sanctum. I do not want you to miss it.

The great naturalist Edwin Way Teale tells in his monumental book, <u>Wandering Through Winter</u>, of the time in

Arizona when he was looking for a hibernating Nuttall's Poorwill, a tiny bird related to the famous Whippoorwill. This rare ornithological treat is usually found nestled in a crevice in the rocks. When Teale finally found one, he was in an area he knew intimately and one that he had crisscrossed time and time again looking for the nuttall. In his book, he observes succinctly, "A thing may be found many times and still be lost. You can walk right by it time and time again. It must be recognized in order to be seen."

Did you get that? You can wander by the very thing you're looking for a thousand times. It is not found; it does not belong to you until you recognize it and claim it as your own. That is where we begin. In Christ's resurrection, a whole new approach to life is offered. It alters everything that ails your individual soul and keeps you at war within yourself.

Charles Cook, a student of the American Church in the late 1960s, announced that he had discovered a new beatitude: "Blessed are they who expect nothing new to happen, for they will not be disappointed." Surely they won't. Billy Graham added that "One of the hardest things to do in this world is to make a Christian out of someone who already thinks he is."

There is a tiny bit of rock in the Pacific Ocean called Easter Island. It is widely known for its massive statues of almost prehistoric human creatures. No one is sure what they stand for or why they were carved out and posted as sentinels along the shore. I have never been there, but some people I have known have visited Easter Island. One of my friends told me that his cruise ship stopped and paid a short visit there as part of a prepackaged tourist destination. He was captivated by it all, even as much as he was mystified. But as he was pondering what it all might mean, he was interrupted by the Captain's mate shouting through a bull-horn, "All aboard! All aboard everybody, we are heading back to the ship!"

That is about enough for Easter Island, but it is not enough about Easter itself. The holiday of which we speak is not an island. It is the mainland of your destination. If you stop and take a quick peek, you will miss the new dimension. You should make the Easter mainland your home forever and a day. You are invited on the journey.

II. Secondly, our text from II Corinthians 5 implies that we can bring Easter to the problems and possibilities of our time. God is a God of history; he is a God who acts. He does not sit idly by watching from the heavens, nor does he sit down to rest when a soul comes forward to surrender to his message. The measure of Easter has an application to the social and community and global problems we face from the day after Easter until it comes back again next year. It must bring some sense of meaning to the one million frantic refugees of Da Nang, some of whom threw their bodies under the wheels of the last plane to leave Viet Nam before the Communists took over. What happens to them now? Each and everyone is a child of God, loved and cared for, just as we are.

And what about the millions here within our own country who are mired in hunger and homelessness? The Easter message must also apply to the myriads who have been disenfranchised by the color of their skin. And what does it say to the 51 percent of us who are working women and who have been passed over, belittled and even abused by the inequalities of the day? The snowfall of the morning must fall in their direction and help cover over the negligence of the past.

Easter must also have a word to speak to the crumbling peace efforts of the Middle East. It must bring some reassurance to those who have been caught in the changing economic conditions of our worn-out way of doing things. It must speak to the poor and the hungry here and all around this wildly spinning planet.

It must also turn inward to the lonely and dispossessed, the fearful and the dying, the guilty and the addicted, and those who are sick or dying from lack of access to decent health care. It must have a decisive word for the liberating ways of Christian theology in this hemisphere, which not only reflects on the processes of the world, but is an integral part of them: God struggling, dying and resurrecting to protest every idiocy of man that tramples human dignity.

To each of them, the proverbial snowfall on Easter morning must blanket all of humanity. It offers respite from the daily struggle. It whispers consoling words to those who are in the final stages of life's journey, to those who will cross the river before the rest of us. Easter brings word that there is an eternal home waiting for each of us, the hope of a new tomorrow.

A few years ago, Peter Berger announced the return to things of the spirit with a marvelous little book called, A Rumor of Angels. The title comes from an incident in the life of a young Roman Catholic priest who was laboring in the slums of a European city to help the poor. Someone asked him why he did it, why he worked so hard for so little. "Why Father, why don't you go to some posh parish in the suburbs? Why do you stay here?" the person asked. "I stay and keep on working, so that the rumor of God will not disappear completely," he responded. Did you hear that? So that the rumor of God's presence will not perish from the earth.

Ah, yes, but it is far more than a rumor. That is why we struggle to make things better than we found them. It is more than a rumor. We are in a time when many try to reduce transcendental treasures to rumors. So be it. The rumor of God's presence is proven here. Our job, then, becomes not so much one of confirming the facts about the Easter stories, but of hanging on to the story and casting the searchlights of our faith on it so that others might see it, too. Easter is not a private message for our eyes only: it is an open letter to the whole wide world.

III. Lastly, Easter whispers its quiet but decisive word in favor of the ones we have loved and lost. It declares the everlasting victory of life over death. The final enemy has been defeated in the death and resurrection of Jesus Christ.

One day we were driving along a delightful country road out by Berwyn, Pennsylvania, when we came across a road sign that said, "You are entering historic Upper Merion Township. Welcome." A while later we read the same sign from the other side. It said, "Goodbye. You are leaving Upper Merion Township. Come back soon." Same sign, two greetings, both authentic.

What you make of it depends on whether you are coming or going. Come by the cross on Good Friday afternoon and you read, "Leaving a Place Called Golgotha: It is finished." But come back the next Sunday morning by the Garden Tomb— the same place, really—and the sign reads, "Welcome. Today

Hell is vanquished. Heaven has won. Come back soon!"

Like a covering of new snow on the face of the dreary earth, it will melt soon enough and the earth will be seen again for what it really is. But from time to time, when we are lucky, we see the other side and behold the glorious rumor coming true that the Lord of all is really here.

"How do you find new worlds anyway?" Archibald MacLeish once asked. "By sailing to them, by crossing mountains, by fording mighty streams – or perhaps by believing in them?" Or perhaps by believing in them. Catch it one last time. Like snowfall on an Easter morning, Resurrection covers all that went before. It transforms your heart and mind and soul and the entire world around us. It puts out the fiery flames; the sting of death is gone. All you need to do is tiptoe up to the Garden, sit down beside the empty tomb and just wait and see. In the name of the Father and the Son and the Holy Ghost, Amen.

IV

THE MIRACLE OF RESURRECTION IN THIS LIFE AND THE NEXT

*"He said to them: "'If they do not hear Moses and the
prophets, neither will they be convinced if someone should
rise from the dead.'"*
LUKE 16:31

This Gospel parable about Abraham and Lazarus in Luke
can get confusing, but it is a marvelous story and useful to our
theme.   It will take you in a new direction to meet "The
Miracle of Resurrection: In this Life and the Next." Here is the
way Jesus told it:

"There was a rich man who was clothed in purple and fine
linen and who feasted sumptuously every day. At his gate lay
a poor man named Lazarus, full of sores, who desired to be fed
with the crumbs which fell from the rich man's table."   It
appears that he did not get many of them. In time, they both
died. The angels carried the poor man straight to heaven, into
the bosom of Abraham. The rich man was buried and went to
hell. It does not say why, although there is more than a hint
that it had to do with his neglect of Lazarus. In the afterlife,
their roles were reversed. The rich man called out to Abraham
from hell where he was in torment. Abraham answered that it

was too late; he could not help him, for an unreachable chasm exists between heaven and hell. Anyway, the rich man had had his share of good things on earth, and Lazarus had none.

The rich man, fearful for the fate of his family members who were still on earth, asked if he could go back and warn his five brothers about what really mattered—apparently to get them to straighten up, fly right and end up rocking in the bosom of Abraham. The rich man and his brothers had heard Moses and the prophets, but they had refused to listen. The rich man said to Abraham, "But if someone comes back to them from the dead to warn them, they will surely listen and will repent," he claimed.

Abraham said, "No, my friend. If they do not hear Moses and the prophets, neither will they be convinced if someone should come back from the dead" (Luke 16:19-31). In other words, a resurrected human coming back to earth would add no weight to what the Torah and the Prophets already had said. It was clear enough without a spectacular rising. End of story.

Now be careful when you try to absorb what the parable means when we come to the Easter resurrection of Jesus. The question is not one of wealth or poverty, and the parable is not really about heaven or hell. The point is that the rich man failed to make the grade and found himself in hell, not because of what he did or had, but because of what he did not do with what he had. That is a fine distinction. However, what was required of him by the Lord God was clear.

It is similar to what St. Paul wrote in Romans: "The wrath of God is revealed from heaven against all ungodliness and wickedness of men who by their wickedness suppress the truth. For what can be known about God is plain to them, because God has shown it to them. Ever since the creation of the world his invisible nature, namely, his eternal power and deity, has been clearly perceived in all things that were made. So they are without excuse; for although they knew God they did not honor him or give thanks to him, but they became futile in their thinking and their senseless minds were darkened. Claiming to be wise, they became fools, and exchanged the glory of the immortal God for images resembling mortal man or birds or animals or reptiles" (Romans 1:18-24).

Paul is working on the same argument as the parable in Luke 16. We have more than enough insight into the ways of the Lord, which have already been revealed in creation. Nature itself, to say nothing of the Scriptures and teachings of the prophets, is sufficient to guide us to the life we should live. The problem is that we fail to live by what we know. We usually know what we should do. The problem is doing it. We have no excuse; pretending to be wise, we become little more than fools unless and until we grasp the truth.

Adding a Resurrection appearance to the picture brings an added dimension if we are thinking about the victory Jesus brought to believers on Easter morning, but it does not add one iota to what we already know about what God requires us to do. People who are not swayed to follow the requirements of the Lord that can be found in nature, the Bible and the individual conscience will not suddenly jump for eternal moral joy and switch over to a new behavior pattern when they hear that Jesus Christ was raised from the dead.

We will go into this matter later in the book, but here we need to return to Jesus' parable of Lazarus and the Rich Man.

Focus on the verse that ends the parable, where it says that if the rich man and his kin were not convinced by Moses and the prophets, they would never be moved to a new life just because someone comes back from the dead. All the proof and impetus needed for a better life are already here on earth.

Our search for a moral-ethical life begins prior to Easter morning. Other bits of revelation have perished along the way. Hope grows old if you allow it, and even love can die. Enthusiasm grays and wanes, marriages get ancient and totter along, and the promise to be good and kind and true is easily set aside. Believe in the Resurrection to Eternal Life, but focus on what it means to be resurrected on earth as well.

Any believing Christian can forget to sing Easter songs come Monday, and the fires to change the world for justice can go flickering out and stop. The spark that flies from the little prayer, "O Lord, keep me alive while I am still living," can generate a new commitment. How we live matters more than how we die. What comes before is more meaningful than what comes after. The life that lies beyond our certitude is a precious hope, but the blinding glory of what heaven is or is not is not our business just yet—that belongs to God alone.

This parable in Luke is our reminder that we should not fasten our Easter vision on the world to come. The desire to belong to Jesus and to give our lives to him usually is combined with our need to be eternally forgiven, which gives us the privilege of trotting up the steps to heaven after Jesus Christ has opened up the gate. We are told that if we believe in his death and resurrection and if we surrender our lives to him and ask forgiveness, we ipso facto cross over to the land of the saved. We are told we will get to heaven, not because we are worth it, or because we have done anything worthwhile, but because we remembered to whisper the few words of the believer's prayer.

After all, we are told, it is God's mercy in Christ alone that allows us to find the Kingdom stairs at all, let alone climb them into paradise. We are saved by grace—sinners redeemed and bought with a price. How exactly we were bought, as if God's forgiveness was up for sale, and what price exactly was paid, is never made quite clear. The Doctrine of the Atonement is being redefined within Christian theology, as it has been many times before. We touched upon this in greater depth earlier in this book. Here we need to ask whether we believe in a vengeful Father God who required the ghastly crucifixion of his own perfect Son, so that the ancient transmitted sin of Adam and Eve could be covered with the proper payment. As familiar as it is, it still sounds strange. Do we worship a Creator God of love who is incapable of forgiving us without allowing the slaughter of his perfectly obedient son?

Meanwhile, we fret and worry over what we cannot comprehend or change. Eye still hath not seen, nor ear heard what the Lord has prepared for us. Even that past master of sentimentality, Alfred Tennyson, mused in his poem In Memoriam that if a deceased friend came back to visit him, he would not believe it; he would be afraid that he had lost his mind and was seeing visions.

If sounds, sights and miracles around us cannot convince us of the love of God, then another miracle will not either. Life is a gift we celebrate. This is the only life we know we have. I repeat: the point of the parable is that we already know what is required, and we all fall short. The living of these days is something that has to be ennobled and renewed. Each and every day we need a mini-resurrection from all that plagues the body and perplexes the soul.

Easter is the Christian festival supreme. Unfortunately, for most it does not last. One reason why it fades is that we assign the resurrection miracle to the future or the past. Either we revel in it as an event that took place in the Garden Tomb, or we reserve it for the moment of our death, when we think we can swipe our Christian card at the turnstile and be admitted. What resurrection really means in this life is that God's creative power can raise us up to something new, so that we can repeat the miracle of new life where it is most needed in the world. We need not argue what the Resurrection was, or what our private resurrection will be someday in the future. We need to raise up something new and resurrect the parts and pieces of human pain which are broken off and dying right before our eyes. We all have seen what happens when the love of God is let loose in the world: people are born again in the compassionate ways of Christ himself. The gift of salvation is not so much a free pass across the final river, but rather a command to share our new lives with others, beginning right now.

Professor H. A. Williams, to whom I am indebted for the title of this chapter, wrote that the problem takes on a special character when we come to the resurrection of the body. We need to open ourselves up and banish the dual mind-body syndrome from our lives. We need a miracle, not a formula or prescription, to end the problems of the soul. Only God can change a heart. We need to love ourselves and allow that self to be renewed in order to move out and change the world.

The beast within our body rages on. No matter what we do or how we change, the lion often rules the lamb. The least that we can do is unplug our ears and shake our souls so we can hear the voice of the Eternal Word in the things that turn us upside down and inside out. At whatever age we are, we must be alert to ourselves, alert for change and newness and be open to the promises and the surprises of the Lord. When we begin to seek, Jesus promises, we will begin to find.

Dr. Williams goes on to say that we are afraid because our bodies are weak and fragile, and we know that the world will keep on going after we are gone. We stumble around in our fear as we deny ourselves the abundant life Christ has promised us. Yet we do not need to wait to find the eternal self; it is already here. We need the blood which courses through our veins, carrying enough oxygen to keep it going smoothly. But it can be so easily interrupted. Life is fragile, but it is the only life we have. What oxygen is to the lungs, Emil Brunner wrote, such is hope to the meaning of human life.

The miracle of being given life beyond the grave is no greater than the miracle of being given life here on earth. The birth of a child is no less a miracle that the beginning of life in eternity, and the gift of new life each day is no less a miracle than either.

That is what the symbol of the Resurrection means—calling into being again a life which was gone. It is an exceptional miracle. But, the greatest miracle of all is Creation itself. In Genesis I, God made the universe out of nothing. Then man and woman were created to walk upon it and to have dominion over it. But what kind of dominion was it intended to be? Who was supposed to have power over whom and what? The earth still belongs to the Creator God. We have a transitory presence while we march ourselves around it, as if we owned it all. But the earth does not belong to us; neither does eternity.

The way the Bible tells the story, heaven and earth both belong to God, who chose to give the keys to his kingdom to Jesus Christ, his son, our Lord. It is up to him to unlock the gates to paradise. It is not our prerogative to decide who goes to heaven and who does not. That is the privilege of the Lord alone. If he chooses to open the gates to those we would deny entrance because they do not meet our formulae, they will enter anyway. Jesus the Christ is the Lord of life and death and eternity. If Jesus chooses to open wide the gates to heaven and admit all children of the Lord God Almighty, what is that to us? Our problem is what to believe and do and say in our mortal life here on earth.

We argue about whether it was an actual physical or merely a psychic kind of resurrection that first Easter. We also speculate how Jesus could ever have raised Lazarus from the dead after he had been gone from life for four days. We wonder what happened to the resurrected body of Lazarus after he was raised by Jesus. Meanwhile, greeting us at daybreak each and every morning is the master miracle, far greater in power than all the others put together: the miracle of the universe itself. God created life out of cosmic dust! The stars were set in their courses and the birds learned to fly. Nothing can match the miracle it took to lay the foundations of the world.

One day I was talking with a man in Kirkcaldy who worked in the coal mines during World War II. During one period, he had to work in the pits for days on end, unburying the precious product to power the mills and warm the homes and keep the fires of freedom burning all over Britain. As the year wore on, he never saw the light of day from fall through winter into early spring. He trundled out in the morning dark, took the lift two miles down into the mine, did his job, and by the time he came up again to head home, it was already dark.

"But when Easter Sunday morning came that year, it was a glorious treat to see the beauty of the shining sun and to hear the message in song and word about how Christ conquered the darkness of the world. I think about it often, and I will never forget that Easter," he said. When you are in the dark, grimy, murky deep and things close in on your sagging spirits, when you don't know where to turn, you need an Easter morning. You need this miracle of resurrection to see the sun shine and bring you hope. You need a Resurrection morning now! Today! Tomorrow! And the next day, too.

Time after time, as we go about our daily business we can see a lovely touch of resurrection here, there and anywhere, if we allow it. The world is full of the rhythm of returning spring, and the quintessential newness that we celebrate in Christ is always waiting just around the corner. I see it in the eyes of little children, in the reminiscences of the oldest people I know, and in everyone in between.

When a congregation has stumbled through the doldrums of petty discontent, when Christian people take sides against their fellow Christians, it is burdensome. But when the newness of God's love comes flooding into the pews and wiggles down between two very different worshippers, when the power and peace found in the presence of the living Christ comes into our lives, all discontent is blown away. I call that a resurrection.

Or when a family stumbles and falls over a disappointment or broken promise or plain and simple boredom, and the love of God comes wandering into this broken home and makes it right again, I call that a resurrection.

A teenager I once knew lost his way and did not know how to find it. Then a friend shared the gift of God by listening, talking and holding out a helping hand. I call that a resurrection.

I knew a wife and mother who awakened one morning feeling that her life was passing her by and she was growing older and had little to show for it. Then God came by and restored her sense of humor and set things right again. I call that a resurrection.

Or what about the husband who became desolate after an accident took away his young bride? He talked as if he intended to join her. Then he met a lovely widow, and the gift of love was soon shining on both their faces. Oh, you should have seen him! I could see the love from a hundred yards away. I call that a resurrection.

How about the successful pastor I knew, who gave up his comfortable parish and went into the ghettos of the city to minister to those who had nothing but need? When he began to touch their lives and help them move up a notch or two, spiritually and economically, I call that a resurrection.

There was a fine young woman in my previous parish who came up to me following a sermon I had preached on the courage Christ required of us. She told me she was quitting her job and going to Africa for two years to serve in the Peace Corps, where she would live and work in the jungle among people without sufficient potable water or desirable food. The family man in me wanted to tell her not to take my preaching too seriously, but when she returned from her tour of duty and shared the news of all she had accomplished, I called that a resurrection.

And when a whole minority people — black, Hispanic, Indian, or any nationality or race — begins to look at itself with pride and breaks the bindings of the past, even when it takes a nasty face of protest, I call that a resurrection. Minorities cannot wait to be resurrected in Heaven; they need a resurrection here and now.

And the people of our nation, with our sagging spirits and aching hearts for all that has slipped away, when the darkness lifts and the doomsday rants are quieted, we will have another resurrection.

For there is inside of me a fundamental belief that the future of America is indispensable to the future of the world. God called us into being when the world had need of us, to move the universe of the people of the earth a little closer to his goal and purpose. Did I not believe that our way of life will ultimately prevail, I would fly off to another planet and affix Dante's Inferno greeting at the door: "Abandon hope, all ye who enter here!"

You need not feel abandoned. The power to work wonders is within ourselves, and when the day comes when we realize we have conquered, whether now or a thousand years from now, we will have a Resurrection! The question is not whether there will be a Resurrection, but whether you have opened up the shades to see the morning light and let the sun shine in. Of course there was a Resurrection, there are resurrections every day and there will be a final Resurrection! The question is whether you allow yourself to see it, and feel it, and love it and live it. Biblical scholars can study the first Easter morning; God in Christ will take care of your Resurrection to eternal life; but you and I must take care of resurrection here on earth.

From the first page of Genesis in which the Spirit of God moves over the face of the deep turning darkness to light, until the last page of the Book of Revelation, where it promises that we will have no need of candles or the light of the sun, and in everything in between, the Spirit of God was, is and will be there to hold our human life and history.

The blessed dead are gone; they are with the Lord. But the Lord is with us, too, within the time and space we occupy. When we die, we do not meet another Lord. We have already met the Creator. The same God is in command of the living and the dead. Our days on earth are but a shadow: three score and ten, and they are gone. We all must perish. But as the departed live on in the house of the Lord, we live with the Risen Christ on all our daily rounds.

In I Corinthians 15, St. Paul writes that if we have hope in Christ for this life only, we are to be pitied. But the opposite is also true: if we have hope only for the next life, and we rest our hope there rather than here, our days on earth become a sham, and we are to be pitied too. If in this life we know that each day lived in the grace of God brings us opportunity to share the love we have been given, if we are resurrected along the way, then we can rest in peace when nightfall comes. "In every wink of an eye, some new grace is born."

As Abraham said to the rich man, you do not need proof in the form of someone returning to tell you what it is like over there, or what you must do here. You have all the proof and information you need. "God is not dead," Harvey Cox once said. "He has gone silent, waiting patiently to hear what you have to say." So say what you believe, then step out to prove it. For now and forever more, Amen.

V

MY LORD, WHAT A MORNING!

*"And very early on the first day of the week they went
to the tomb when the sun had risen, . . ."*

MARK 16:2

Every spring the Three Rivers Arts Festival comes to downtown Pittsburgh. Culture blossoms out all over the place in a bright and welcomed extravaganza of painting and poetry and music and drama and sculpture and all the other arts. Invited artists display their talents in the lobbies of corporate buildings, on the streets, in the park, and even on the sides of buses. Meanwhile, music and poetry readings and dramas are presented on stages tucked into every nook and cranny around the city. Painters finish canvasses, sculptors sculpt and metal artists use their blow torches to weld their works together right in front of your eyes.

One day early in the festival, an artist from New England appeared with unusual skills. Gifted with chalk pastels, he entertained the passing public by sketching lovely pictures on the concrete sidewalks, just like any kid would do it, only better. His pastel scenes were beautiful, and it was an incredible treat to watch a grown-up boy on his hands and knees draw portraits and still life scenes in chalk on the sidewalk.

Artists usually hope their works will last forever, like cavemen's carvings and ancient sculptures. Usually it does not happen, but with the sidewalk artist, the creation barely lasted through the evening. The crowds eventually walked over his treasures, or the evening rains washed them away. I have often thought about the transitory nature of such an occupation. The memory of it has followed me for decades. While it missed the quality of permanence, it affirmed the importance of the moment— an idea that reigned during the early years of that festival. It also reflected what we have come to believe about many sacred objects and ideas. I asked the chalk artist why he worked that way. "My art is for the moment," he replied. "That is all we really know we have." True, as spoken.

Others have said the same about the creation itself, about human life and about the afterlife. "What you see is what you get," is a normal mantra. "Why look for more?" Some envision God as a kind of grown-up kid playing games, creating the universe and life for some existential sport, only to be washed away the moment the next cosmic rain falls down on this portion of the universe.

The chalk artist introduction is a perfect segue into the subject of this chapter. I write here about the gift of life, about what God has prepared, and about the salient significance of the Resurrection of Jesus Christ. There are four reasons why you and I can and should believe the message of Easter and the eternal significance of human life. Faith is always a gift, and having received it from God, there are some important foundation stones that can be used to hold it up in any company.

I. First, Biblical evidence supports the Resurrection of Jesus Christ from the dead. That statement may annoy believing Christians, but I emphasize that intense examination of Scripture is imperative before we can return to the believer's simple Easter conclusion. The evidence comes primarily from the Gospel records and from St. Paul. Outside the New Testament, there are only two isolated historical references to the Resurrection, both of which report it simply as being believed by Christians. Matthew, Mark, Luke, John and The Letters of St. Paul are the only primary sources.

To some readers, the Biblical testimony will automatically become a final positive proof. "If the Bible says it, it is true and I must and will believe it." Seldom do such outspoken believers explain how they came to know what they think they know about the Bible, nor do they have good answers for the questions about variations in the Scripture, some of which are confusing or close to contradiction.

From another angle, many reject the Gospels without a second look. They say that the Holy Bible is but one of many ancient religious books belonging to a pre-scientific era that tries to cast its mortal light on immortal and eternal verities. One doctor friend of mine calls the Old Testament "a batch of fairy stories." Perfectly sane, sensible, kind and thoughtful people, seeking to find the truth of God and man, will not allow their minds to rest just because the things they read in the Bible "ain't necessarily so." I am aware that trying to understand and prove the Resurrection from the New Testament will not carry the same weight of finality with everyone.

However, I press on. There are no serious disagreements regarding the Resurrection anywhere in the New Testament.

The four Gospel writers differ in various details concerning when it happened, who was present, what they found, who they saw, and how the Lord went up to heaven. But they are unanimous in agreeing that it happened.

In Luke, curiously, Jesus never appears at all on Easter morning. The angel at the tomb simply tells the women that he has gone away. In a kind of afterthought in Chapter 23, which may have been added to Luke sometime after the Gospel was written, the Risen Lord appears to Cleopas and another follower on the Road to Emmaus.

In Mark, three women come to the Sepulcher; in Matthew there are two women, and in John, Mary Magdalene came alone. Some of the Easter day appearances occur in Jerusalem and some in Galilee, and they seem to overlap, even though there is a distance of 75 to 80 miles between these cities.

Later, St. Paul makes reference to the 500 brethren who saw Jesus at one time, but no further explanation of that visit is recorded in the Gospels. By the time the Gospels were written — say a dozen or more years after Paul's epistles — such an event would have been widely known.

Also the story of Thomas and his doubts is so common that he is often called Doubting Thomas, but Matthew says that many others doubted when they went out to meet him on the mountain as he was about to ascend to heaven (Matthew 28:17).

According to the Gospel composite story, something monumental occurred on that Saturday night or early Sunday morning. There is obvious disagreement about when and how the Tomb was opened and how the stone got rolled away. It is not clear what the soldiers guarding the tomb did and said. Only Matthew includes them in the story. There is some agreement, even among the enemies of Jesus, that the tomb was empty. Some claimed his body was stolen, and others said it was transferred to a new place.

So what happened? If the Pharisees or their hired hands had removed the body, and either they or the Romans had reburied it somewhere outside the Garden, it surely would have been exhumed and brought to the Village Square when the growing enthusiasm of the new religion began to circulate. Whoever took it and laid it away so the Disciples could not get it would have produced it on a moment's notice to prove that the King of the Jews was really dead.

On the other hand, if the Disciples had stolen it (a most unlikely possibility, for they were powerless and scared to death), it hardly seems possible that a group of devoted followers would live with such conviction and die with such courage knowing that they had taken the body and it was all a hoax. No one in his right mind would face the lions in the Arena, or die by the gladiator's sword, knowing that the touchstone of their new faith was a lie. The empty tomb was never their reassurance anyway: they found their faith in the words of the Angel and in the appearances of Jesus.

Ten post-resurrection appearances of Jesus are recorded in the New Testament. He often came in a transfigured form, but was usually recognizable. Those he visited knew who he was, even when it took a little while. He ate food with them, and he invited them to touch the wounds of his hands and side. In the last analysis, however, the evidence from Scripture still leaves some uncertainty as to exactly what happened.

One problem is that two separate traditions converge in the Gospels, reflecting two then contemporary ways of looking at death and eternal life. We are not the first generation to ponder these issues. At that time, the Pharisee's tradition believed in the resurrection of the body, just as Christians do today. St. Paul was trained as a Pharisee. Others believed that while the body decays and returns to dust, the spirit (or soul) survives the finality of death. Not unlike today, the Pharisees and the Sadducees argued over whether one would awaken and be raised in body, or whether one would be lifted up in a spiritual type of everlasting life.

In Genesis, man and woman were created when God breathed into them, and they became "living souls," i.e., the body and soul combined into one being. The separation of body and soul is not an Old Testament idea; it was borrowed from Greek and Roman philosophy. The Gospel Resurrection stories include both reigning views regarding resurrection: Jesus is both a resurrected body and an exalted spirit, but in him these two are joined together.

St. Paul complicates the matter further. When he refers to the post-Resurrection appearances of Christ, he groups all sightings together. In I Corinthians 15, he writes that Jesus appeared to the disciples, to Peter, to an unknown group of 500, "and last of all, he appeared to me." Paul is referring to the vision he had of Jesus on the road to Damascus. He does not appear to be worried about separating a physical presence from the vision in which he had heard the voice of Jesus.

Mark, the earliest Gospel, leaves Easter morning in healthy mystery. In the original edition of Mark, the women who went to the tomb and found it empty were deeply afraid and told no one that they had not found the body of the Lord. This implies that Jesus might have ascended directly into heaven on or before the sun rose. It would have been a resurrection of the body itself: if the spirit or soul of Jesus had left his body and floated up to heaven, the body would have remained in the tomb.

It should not alarm believing Christians that Biblical accounts differ. If everyone agreed on all details, they would be accused of having been coached so their stories would be consistent. The records are fresh and new; they reveal bewilderment and awe and wonder. They differ, but there was obviously no conspiracy to fabricate a believable story. It was all too magnificent and marvelous for words to express. The writers were overcome and lost in the bewilderment of the morning. It was as novel to them as it is to us.

II. The second thing we notice is that the early Church came to believe the Easter story. That is not as obvious as it sounds. Every time the extraordinary impinges on our ordinary ways of doing things, there is always a difference of opinion as to what happened and whether or not it could be true. Each time heaven breaks into the earthly realm, fear results, as it did with the shepherds in the fields and Mary in her room.

People ask me time and again if what they have experienced was real. One intelligent, well-balanced parishioner asked if it were possible that he really had heard the voice of his departed wife, or was he going crazy? "I had a vision of white light passing through a long tunnel and emerging on the other side, where I saw my husband and other friends and family members who were dead. Please tell me, Dr. Cromie, was it true, or was it a figment of my imagination? Was it a dream, or was the Lord reassuring me of heaven?" she asked.

Early in my ministry, I was not sure how to answer such

questions. I was puzzled by the contradictions. Later, I learned not to try to settle everything within the bounds of my rational experience. I became more open to what others said and told me that they saw. Others would say that such paranormal experiences are simply projections of the brain and psyche. Just as many would tell you they are true.

So, it is not surprising that some who were present doubted that they saw the Risen Christ. It was too overwhelming—too unbelievable. And yet the Church came to believe it—chose to believe it, I should say—and that is significant. Surely the Disciples were just as intelligent, healthy, sane and diverse as we are, and their belief transformed them. In the conviction that Jesus the Christ had risen from the dead, they found the courage to go on.

Without that conviction, I think it is fair to say that there would have been no Church, no Reformation, no Western civilization, no missionary movement, no abiding concern for health and education and human dignity, and no antidote to hatred and to death. Christianity has heralded these advancements in our world. Evil would have triumphed. If Christ was not raised, our faith would be in vain. It is all related to where and how they found their power in their conviction that the Resurrection happened. There are other explanations to be sure; but I choose to believe this one.

A lie cannot keep you courageous and stalwart while wrestling with lions, nor take you through the persecutions of 19 centuries. A lie does not have the power to persuade you not to recant your belief in Jesus Christ when you are faced with the same fires that consumed the martyrs of old. A lie may live in a jungle, but as the followers of Jim Jones found in Honduras, poisoned grape Kool-Aid can wash it away in less than a decade. The testimony of the early disciples and all others who have followed gives authenticity to the story.

If I were a nonbeliever, the greatest obstacle I could imagine would be the conviction of the disciples and others believers whose lives were transformed by the Resurrection. Sure, there are good and intelligent people who do not believe in the Resurrection. On the other hand, there are millions of marvelous, deep, intelligent people who do. No one should be ashamed to embrace the miraculous power and presence of the Lord. We have said that Biblical evidence supports it, and the disciples and their descendants have believed it.

III. Thirdly, the resurrection is compatible with the other things we know about the mysterious way in which God works with his created beings. "Lo, I tell you a mystery," says Paul about the Resurrection. But what is a mystery anyway? It technically means, "Relating to the ways of God, beyond human comprehension." A mystery is inscrutable, incompletely known, as the mystery of the Eucharistic presence of the Lord. The Creator God normally deals with us in mystery: "Your thoughts are not my thoughts," says the Lord. "Neither are your ways my ways."

More informally, a mystery is something you know happened, but you are not sure how. This is true whether on a magician's stage or on the grand stage of life. Whatever explanation we give for understanding the vast evolutionary process we call Creation, we know little of the "how" and nothing of the "why." Christ's birth was surrounded by mystery; virgin births just do not happen. How did the Wise Men know to follow the guiding star? How can you follow a star?

Our lives from birth to love to death are full of mystery. The mystery of the open door to the empty tomb belongs in the same stream of what we know and what we believe. Is it a greater mystery that life should keep on keeping on than it is that life began in the first place? God did not roll the dice and make life on a whim. It is just like Him to offer a tiny peek over the top of the mountain, a tease that makes you say, "Wow! How did He do that?"

It is as if God were saying, "Lo, I tell you a mystery. I will share it with you. I will give you a quick peek. Ready? It's gone." Annie Dillard wrote in her beloved Pilgrim at Tinker Creek, "I blinked my eyes this spring, and I missed it all again." It touches on the way God reveals himself to us. Pay attention.

The Resurrection brings you one word you need to hear: Victory. We need reassurance at the edge of an open grave. We need to believe in the sun, even when it is not shining, in love when we do not feel it, and in forgiveness when it is not received.

In All the Strange Hours, my old friend Loren Eiseley told the story of a professor friend at a small observatory in northern Montana. Jim Radnor was a good man with a gift of imagination, but he had this quirk: He believed there had once been a planet in the wide gap of space between Jupiter and Mars. He speculated that it had exploded into bits and flown away. Every night, he wandered up to his observatory and trained his telescope into space, peering hopefully into the emptiness, searching for the interplanetary bones of a planet now gone.

Loren asked him one day why he did it. "Radnor, if there were a missing planet out there somewhere, someone would have surely found it. Every telescope on earth penetrates into the deepest recesses of the galaxy, and no one has found the remnants of your planet." Radnor said, "There are asteroids out there, Loren, moving where there should be a planet. And I know why no one found it; they are not looking for it. They are all looking for something else. Someday I will find it; someday I will have it in my line of sight."

We need more watchers for Easter morning too. We need more people looking at the heavens as Christians did from the early years through the Dark and Middle Ages. They went out at 3:00 a.m. on Easter morning and prayed and waited and watched for the morning. When it finally came, the cannon would boom, bands would strike up and the people would sing, "My Lord, what a morning! My Lord, what a morning when the stars began to fall ..."

When the end comes, when the Lamb who was slain unravels the scroll of life, when the stars and the planets leave their respective places and the moon and sun go to dark for good, when all that is hidden is finally made known, oh what a great happy morning that will be!

Meanwhile, the news you need to hear is waiting for you this very moment. You had better hurry, or you might miss it. It arrived in Jerusalem one morning two thousand years ago, while most of the old city was still asleep. The last enemy was met and conquered that night: Christ died and was raised by God from the dead. Everything is going to be okay.

You need something to help you believe that life is more than chalk marks on streets, more than something temporary that will be washed away by the next rain or rubbed to ruin. You need to know that your life and the lives of those you love are in his tender care and keeping. You need reassurance from

Christ himself. Are you looking for the truth that God wants to share with you this happy, holy morning? I hope so, for now and for ever more. Amen.

VI

THE MAN WHO MISSED EASTER

"I am the Resurrection, and the Life. . ."
JOHN 11:25

It happened one Easter evening as I was ambling home from a little walk around the neighborhood where we lived. When I got back to my driveway, our next door neighbor was pulling into his. Jim was a tough man to love. He hardly ever spoke to anyone, and when he did, it was series of low grunts and growls. Children, dogs and ladies crossed over to the other side of the street when old Jim came passing by. I had met him one morning a couple of years earlier, and we struck up what you might call a mini-friendship. Maybe it was just that Jim grunted more softly at me. He had never uttered a kind word to anyone, at least not since the day his wife had suddenly died and their children did not come home for the funeral. That was the day I met him.

Anyway, as he pulled his Oldsmobile into the driveway that

Easter evening, I waved and called over:

> "Hi, neighbor,"
> "Hullo, Rev,"
> "How are you, Jimmy boy?"
> "Fine, How ya doin'?"
> I said, "I'm tired . . . had a busy day." (It was Easter
> Sunday, after all.)
> "Oh?" he said.

"Yeah, I was up at 5:00 to get ready for the Sunrise Service. Then I preached at 9:00 and 11:00, visited some shut-in parishioners to give them the Sacrament, then my wife and I entertained both of our families for Easter dinner. I'm bushed. Time to call it a day."

Jim looked at me astonished; his glasses slipping a little down his nose. His forehead furrowed, and the corners of his mouth drew in. "R-r-rev, w-w-was this Easter?" he stuttered with pathetic incredulity. I smiled and nodded. He said, "Oh my God, I missed it. What a darn dumb thing to do." It turned out that he had driven over to Ohio, had a little lunch, had walked around a lake they used to know, and came home, just like any other Sunday. Poor Jim. It was Easter, and he missed it!

There's humor in that story to one who plans Easter six months in advance, and sees the Paschal Morning as the most important day in the history of the world. It is hard to imagine how someone could miss Easter.

The Biblical backdrop to this chapter is a scene from John 11, in which Jesus came to Bethany to be with his friends Mary and Martha, whose brother Lazarus had died. The Gospel says Jesus loved Martha and her brother Lazarus. The family had sent word that Lazarus was "sick unto death," but for reasons which are not clear, Jesus delayed his visit until after Lazarus had been dead four days.

When he arrived, Martha tells him that if he had been there, her brother would not have died. Jesus replies that her brother will rise again. She thinks he is referring to the resurrection on the last day, when all who have fulfilled the Law of Torah will rise into eternity. But Jesus says to her, "I am the Resurrection and the Life. They who believe in me, though they die, yet shall they live, and whoever lives and believes in me shall never die." Jesus then turns to Martha and said, "Do you believe it?" And she says, "Yes, Lord, I believe" (John 11: 17-27).

There is the good news of Easter: that Jesus Christ is risen from the dead; that God can conquer all our sins and worries and fears of life and death. He can also transform all that is dead in your life, and recreate it, making it fresh and new again.

Jesus was not speaking about a resurrection of a soul or spirit which occupies our bodies and then flies off somewhere to heaven. He was referring to a resurrection of The Body— the total person. It is not so much that our human frame will regroup and live again, but that we will be recognizable persons, a concept that is taught in the Old and New Testaments and one in which the Church still believes.

Some other faiths believe in a reincarnation of the spirit, in an eternal soul which survives individual death of the body and returns back again and again in a higher or lower form of life each time around, depending on how well or poorly the previous one was lived. In that view, the human body is merely a resting place, a temporary repository in which the eternal spirit abides while on Planet Earth.

Reincarnation is a captivating idea, but one I cannot reconcile to my Christian Faith. It seems to explain why some people have such a cruel fate in life. If you are being punished for what happened in a previous generation, it makes sense that bad things can happen to bad people. But the concept is alien to the incarnation of God in Jesus and to the creation of Adam and Eve in the image of God, each a complete person, not a body that a wandering spirit inhabits for a while.

Belief in the Christian "resurrection of the body" is a difficult concept, hard to comprehend and fraught with many dangers and misunderstandings. St. Paul had already discovered that when he wrote to the Corinthians, who were also puzzled. Paul writes, "Some will ask, 'How are the dead raised? With what kind of body do they come?' You foolish people! What you sow does not come to life unless it dies. And what you sow is not the body which is to be, but a bare kernel, perhaps of wheat or some other grain. God gives it a body as he has chosen, and to each kind of seed its own body. … There are celestial bodies and there are terrestrial bodies; but the glory of the celestial is one, and the glory of the terrestrial body is another. There is one glory of the sun, and another glory of the moon, and another glory of the stars; for stars differ from stars in glory. So it is with the resurrection of the dead. What is sown is perishable, what is raised is imperishable. It is sown in dishonor, it is raised in glory. It is sown in weakness, it is raised in power. It is sown a physical body, it is raised a spiritual one."

Paul concludes: "Lo! I tell you mystery. We shall not all sleep, but we shall be changed in a moment, in the twinkling of an eye, at the last trumpet. ... For this perishable nature must put on the imperishable, and this mortal nature must put on immortality ... then shall come to pass what is written: 'Death is swallowed up in victory.' O death, where is thy victory? O death, where is thy sting?" ...Thanks be to God, who gives us the victory through Jesus Christ our Lord." (I Corinthians 15: 35-56 RSV)

Paul's words are helpful, but on closer look, they do not answer the question completely. He resorts to images and metaphors to elevate the subject to a higher level. He is sure the body that will be raised is not the same body that dies. Everyone knows that a frail and fragile body disappears instantly in flames or over time in the earth. It is a mortal body. But Paul explains there is also an immortal body, no more like the one that dies than the waving fields of wheat are like the seeds which are planted in the ground. We will be raised to a celestial newness, incorruptible and imperishable.

Over the years I have fielded many questions about the resurrection of the body. What kind of body is it? What age will I be in heaven? What will happen to my infant child, will he be a three-week-old forever? Will my husband be waiting for me? What will happen to my decrepit, aching body? Especially as we grow older, we can all understand Liston Pope who said, "The idea that I might go on being me forever is too dreadful to contemplate."

We need to listen again to St. Paul, who understood that we will not have the same body in the afterlife as we have here and now. But we need not inquire too rigorously, demanding detailed answers to our specific questions. If St. Paul can rest in images and similes and metaphors, so can we. If you get all bogged down in the details, you will miss Easter as surely as my neighbor did the Sunday he drove over to Ohio. I do not want you to miss it.

The Christian Church believes in the resurrection of Christ's body, not alone in the endurance of his Spirit. Some believe that the soul or spirit of Jesus was raised again to wander around the earth, and some time later floated back to heaven. They call it a "spiritual resurrection." It might sound more logical, but it falls short of the full message of the Gospel: "If Christ is not raised, our faith is in vain."

The Gospel writers do not agree on all the details: they, too, were searching for the meaning of it all. They were puzzled about this mysterious occurrence, but each and every one grasped the message. There is mystery about it all, but there is no mystery whatever about the victory of life over death.

There are concerns about the resurrection of the body. The Risen Body of Jesus did not last on earth forever. He ascended into Heaven and is sitting on the right hand of God. It is imperative to believe that each of us will remain recognizable in heaven as the same people we are on earth. We will be released from all that binds us to our mortal frame. We shall live forever, and forever is a long, long time. But I will still be I, and you will still be you.

The earliest renditions of the Gospels tell how the women and the Disciples found an empty tomb. They were reassured Christ was no longer there in the grave. He was risen, as he said he would be. In Mark, the earliest Gospel, the ascension into heaven seems to have taken place immediately. Mark does not report a single post-resurrection appearance of Jesus. He does not deny them, but if he knew about them, it seems he would have talked about them at the conclusion of his story. Some editions of the Bible, including the widely used King James Version, include Mark 16:9-20 as part of the original Gospel itself. Since the subject matter of Mark 16:9-20 is fully covered in the other three Gospels, nothing of importance was added later. But we have come to know that these verses were not in the earliest versions of Mark.

Nothing written here is intended to denigrate our faith. I believe in the Resurrection of Jesus. But in attaching faith to details, you can miss the larger possibilities. The least plausible explanation of all is that the Disciples' faith was based on some trick they conjured up. They, too, were incredulous. And you cannot assume they were naïve or superstitious. On the whole, they were as intelligent and inquisitive as those who dissect their stories now.

The Disciples were not preconditioned to believe that people were created so that their bodies would return to life after they died. Adam and Eve were apparently promised that they would live forever, unless they took of the tree of original sin – at least, that is what Eve told the serpent God had said. But after their sin of disobedience, the gift of eternal life was rescinded.

There is good news for those who are prepared to hear it, and there is victory for those who are ready to claim it in Christ. Many people missed it then, and so many miss it now! Most of Jerusalem missed it that first morning, when their lives returned to normal. "Ho, hum, another Passover over and done," they thought. The moneychangers at the Temple missed it. They had been peeved that week when a fanatic from Galilee had stomped into the temple grounds and kicked over their tables, screaming his fool head off and driving their customers away. But it was merely a brief and awkward interlude; by the first day of the week they were busy again counting money and toting up the profits of a busy holiday season.

Pilate missed it, too. He was so preoccupied with his political position and his duties that he had no time to follow his emotions. He washed his hands of it all: "Enough of this. It's not worth my worry. You take him now and do what you will with him." Pilate missed Easter Sunday morning because he was mapping plans for his career and conjuring up ways to stay in power.

And the church people missed it, too. The believers—Caiaphas and Annas and their fellow ecclesiastics—were quite relieved. "Thank Yahweh, that's the end of that. It was a close call, but we showed him. The threat is over. The Galilean carpenter was proved to be a fraud. His challenge to our proper ways has ended." They were alarmed when they heard that the body of Jesus had disappeared, so they paid off the guards and told them to tell the people that Jesus' disciples had stolen the body. "And this story is spread among the people to this day" (Matthew 28:15).

And Judas missed it. After turning Jesus over to the authorities, his soul and psyche could not bear the weight of his betrayal. For 30 pieces of silver, he betrayed the best friend he ever had. Pity poor, dumb, mercenary Judas Iscariot, who could not stand such goodness in his midst. But Judas did not betray Christ so much as he betrayed himself. He had it all, and he lost it; he was found hanging from his self-selected gallows, dead and gone two days short of the final victory.

The huge Passover crowd missed it too. Some historians guess that Passover week brought more than a quarter million visitors to Jerusalem. That is a lot of people. But on the first morning of the week, they were packing up, finishing arrangements to get their goods and family members back home; or they had already gone.

And the company of fellow pilgrims who had followed Jesus into town missed it, too. They had wandered off in grief, wondering how the authorities could have been so cruel to someone so kind and loving, and how stupid they were to have been duped by a would-be savior. They were bewildered and let down that this horrid thing had happened. The Bible says they were afraid and puzzled and tentative, so most of them fled, or at least departed for their appointed places.

The women close to Jesus also missed it for a while. Their eyes were too filled with tears to see. They wanted to perform their little chores, the set routines of grief, and embrace the emptiness so they could know a specific enemy.

And incredibly, some of his closest confidants missed it, too. Matthew writes, "The eleven disciples went out with him to the mount of Galilee and when they saw him"— the Risen Lord that is — "they worshipped him, but some of them doubted." Can you believe it? They saw him standing right in front of them. Peter, Andrew, James and John fell on their knees to worship him, yet some of the others could not believe their eyes and ears.

So many people missed it, and I am afraid that some of you will miss it, too. We get so confounded busy in our own ways of doing God's work, carefully delineating what and where we will serve, mediating God's own grace through the narrow channels of our preferences. We become weary, or we get miffed. I heard about a woman who ruined Easter for herself and her family because she didn't like the way the Easter lilies were arranged on the altar.

Some miss it because they cannot believe it. They are so bright and logical that they sit in judgment on matters of our faith. They say, "Dead men do not rise up and walk the earth again. We need proof, not the meager testimony of the biased." They wonder why he appeared only to those who believed in him? Was it their reward? Why didn't he go over to Rome and rap on Caesar's front door, they query? Why didn't he drop by the palace of Pontius Pilate and show him the Truth in person?" Some cannot let themselves linger around the empty grave for too long; they fear someone or something might penetrate the shell of their intellectual excellence.

I will say it softly, but if you listen carefully, you will hear the challenge: Turn it loose. You need to walk the misty mountains that take your breath away, up where you can see the past and into the future. You're not so tough, just because you're bright and got good grades in school. No one is graded here. Be open to the surprises of the Lord. Don't let your big brain get in the way of what you need. In the end, it is child-like faith that matters.

Others will miss it today because they are so preoccupied with their own problems. Whatever your worries are, you need an Easter morning. Your grief, your aging, your faltering marriage, your concern for loved ones, your worries about yourself, your fears for the future of the world, all these can take a ride on the wings of Easter morning. Don't miss it because your heart, mind and soul are wedded to your own heap of troubles.

And we are missing some other things as well, you know. Marvelous things are happening these days. Great and mighty plans are being laid to help to set the stage for the victory of Christ on earth. Churches are on the move. Battles are being waged for brotherhood and sisterhood and peace and poverty and hunger and justice and equality. Great things are happening to help people cross the boundaries of race and sex and age. I do not want my Christian friends to miss them. Remember Washington Irving's novel, <u>Rip Van Winkle</u>? Rip fell asleep for 20 years and missed the entire American Revolution. When he finally got up to do something about it, it was over.

The other day, as I read the Resurrection stories for the umpteenth time, the final words of Luke jumped out at me as if I had never read them before. When it was all over, after the empty tomb, after Jesus' appearances, after Emmaus, after the week when Jesus had appeared to the Disciples and showed them the nail holes in his hands and the spear hole in his side, Luke says the Resurrected Christ opened up their minds to understand the Scripture. He told them that he had to suffer, and now that it was time for him to go, it was their time to preach repentance and forgiveness to all the nations on earth. He was returning to eternity. From that moment on it was up to his followers to be his witnesses.

Even on Easter Sunday morning, we note the powerful message that our Lord was sharing. Everyone needs to hear it. Everyone needs to know it, have it and hold it for their darkest moments. It's up to you and me to do that, friends, to share the story of the Good News of Jesus Christ. And some of you will miss it, too, because you will never take it seriously. You will soon be back into your old routines, the same busyness and the same petty peeves.

According to one of the oldest legends, the sun is said to dance on Easter morning. Up in the hills of northern Italy, they say the sun makes three cheerful little skips at the moment of its rising in honor of the Resurrection of the Lord. It is not too much to say that the very purpose of our lives is to see that little dance on Resurrection morning, to touch and sense and feel and keep and hold forever more the thrill of everything that Easter brings, to know the Good News, which can overcome the doldrums of our time, and skip a beat or two in honor of its rising.

We all need an Easter morning. We need the message that good triumphs over evil, that life triumphs over death. We need to know that all is well and right with the world, not so much because God is in his heaven, but that he is among us here in the form of the Risen Christ. I would not want you to miss it.

I will close this chapter by recalling the time when my wife and I went to Pasadena, California, to attend the Super Bowl. Our favorite team, the Pittsburgh Steelers, was there to compete against the Los Angeles Rams. If you ever lived in Pittsburgh, or know the unbounded devotion of another city to its teams, you will know how privileged we were to be there. A not-so-funny thing happened, however. A young man of 25 or so who had also journeyed to Pasadena for the game was seated just in front of us. Sadly, this boy never saw the game. By the time he stumbled into his seat, the merry-making of the previous hours took their toll, and he slept through the entire game. He never saw a single play of the very game he came to see. He was the envy of his friends back home, and he missed it all. The Steelers won, but he never knew it until the next morning rolled around.

Don't miss it. Each and every one of us needs an Easter Morning. My hope is that everyone on earth will see it, and embrace the victory and carry it with them all their days. That way, my neighbor Jim, the young man in Pasadena, you, I and all God's children everywhere will sing the Easter Wish:

May the glad dawn
of Easter morn
bring joy to thee.

May the calm eve
of Easter leave
a peace of Divine
within thee.

May Easter night
on thine heart write,
O Christ
I live for Thee.

VII

SPRING DOES NOT COME IN A DAY

"He is the image of the invisible God, the first-born of all creation; for in Him all things were created, in heaven and on earth, visible and invisible, whether thrones or dominions or principalities or authorities – All things were created through Him and for Him."

COLOSSIANS 1:15-17

There is something fresh about the spring—in most parts of the country, anyway. When the weather gets hung up on the ridge of winter, and the cold and snow and frost linger far too long into the time the season should change, I remember a sweet, short reminder that my Uncle Bill used to say. It goes, "Spring does not come in a day."

I am writing this in early April, just as the cool rains are about to clean the earth once more. The grass will suddenly turn green, the woods come back to life and the daffodils and the crocus and forsythia will burst into bloom with all their might. Some years it is dreadful when the snow keeps falling and the frost keeps rising, and winter fights to hold its ground. Then the sun comes out and spring is here! Some years it disappears again, and we go back and forth for weeks. I remember an early May when our cottage at Drumrack was covered with snow.

One year we bought a house in mid-November and never saw the roof or ground until Lent was almost over. "There will be Easter surprises aplenty at the morning sunrise service," the weatherman said one Saturday night. He was right: We had to move indoors. It took many years for me to remember that spring does not come in a day, and I still get fooled.

We have lived many different places in the world, but if I am not there to see the changing of the seasons in the Northeast, I miss it. "Spring recapitulates the past," Hal Borland once wrote, "It reminds me of the springtime of life upon this planet" when the world was young and our dependence on nature was more apparent, before we were driven out of the Garden and compelled to make our way through the concrete canyons of the city, in the overpowering loneliness of it all. It has been a long, long time since Demeter's dear Persephone touched the dry brown hills and filled the earth with green. The recreation myths remind us of the power and the presence of spring, but no where does springtime come in a day. Easter is far more than spring—far, far more than sap rising in the trees, or woods blossoming with color or the pleasant aromas after the olfactory desert of winter. The sudden burst of glory that we celebrate on Easter is a treat. But I have come to realize that Easter does not come in a day.

The Resurrection story in the Scripture is a straightforward matter, although not without mystery. According to the Scripture, no one witnessed the Resurrection. It happened in the dark, while Jerusalem slept. The next day, stories began to creep around the town that Christ had risen from his grave.

On that first Easter Sunday, the story circulated that the Disciples had stolen the body and hidden it away. No one really saw it happen and that's a pity. It impinges upon our powerful need for intellectual reassurance. Tantalizing it is, the way it happened. Sometimes its spiritual power overwhelms me; at other times I fight to hold my ground against the questions in my soul.

But it was just like God to do it the way He did; just like the Lord and master of us all, the one by whose power the universe came into being (also a mystery, by the way); just like the one who breathed his breath into a form and it became a living being (that is a mystery, too). God never feels the need to dot our "i's" or cross our "t's." The ways of the Lord are beyond our comprehension.

A little girl once asked me how I knew it all was true. "That what was true?" I asked her. "That Jesus came alive again after he was dead," she said. How do I know it is true? The assertion that the transcendent and eternal God appeared in the body of Jesus to conquer life through his death and resurrection remains essentially a radical statement in the realm of faith.

Of course, we who seek to know it find it to be truer the further we look. But if you try to wrap it up in ordinary parlance, you will be disappointed. One day I can explain it and the next day I am befuddled. Try as I will, it will not fall into step. It is as frustrating as waiting for spring to finally come.

Spring does not come in a day. It took eons to fashion a living man and woman. Step back and ponder the eons it took to get us where we are today. The wonder is not the evil in the world; the wonder is the good we see around us. The wonder is not that things breaks down, but that life was ever built up to become filled with love and faith. The wonder is not that a vast explosion formed the universe, but that the universe managed to form a living, loving person. The ultimate in wonder is not death but life. Like the arrow point of evolution, as Father Teilhard called it, we need to be reminded how far human life has come, not how far we have to go.

In the enormous advances of our modern civilization, we need another kind of basic resurrection. On the centennial anniversary of New York State University, the learned poet Alfred Noyes had the temerity to say, "The first need of modern education is to recover faith in the risen Christ." Do you agree with him? I think he struck a familiar chord with which most of us can harmonize. That could be the very heart of the problem: that Easter is missing from the world. The decline of love, the rise of immorality, the frustrating search for peace, the frantic pace of getting things for ourselves, the preoccupation with trivial matters: all these and many more could explain the rise of human hatred and the domination of less-than-human violence. "They have taken away our Lord," the woman told the men standing by the tomb. So few know where they have laid him.

We have removed the mystery and awe. Our first need is to recover the impetus for life when death was conquered. The choice is a personal one. If it is not true, pray tell me, what is going on? If the message of the moment is not true, then head for the hills and hide, my friends. If there is no surety against the machinations of calumny and hate and tragedies, and no retribution, no balance, no answer, then a madman is in charge, or no one at all, and I want no part of it! If goodness does not ultimately triumph in the universe, then let us abandon faith, turn out the lights and catch as catch can until our days on earth are through.

Ah, but if it is true, if God is playing the game by his own rules, which are unknown to us in part, if he made the world and placed mankind upon it for a purpose, if it is true enough to bet your life on, as Pascal said, then you and I had better give ourselves up to Easter before we all go crazy.

In Lloyd Douglass' novel, <u>The Robe</u>, Marcellus says to Justus, "If you think Jesus is alive, pray tell me, where is he?" Justus shakes his head and says, "I don't know where he is, but I do know he is alive. I don't know where he is, but I'm looking for him all the time. Every time a door opens, at every turning of the road, at every street corner, at the crest of every hill. I don't know where he is, but I do know he is alive and here, and I am always looking for him."

The whole world is asking the question, if Christ is alive, then where on earth is he? Why doesn't he do something to assuage our pain within, to give us some direction to change the course of human life? The saints on earth are hurting, and laughter echoes in the hallways of the wicked. If Christ is alive, if he has power, why does he fail to use it? And as tears stream down our cheeks, the question comes, "O God, why? Where are you?"

Now and then, we feel his presence and know that he is near. In our better moments, we can cross the great divide and accept the gift of resurrection. I have my deep convictions, even if they waver from time to time. I don't know where he is, either, but I believe he is in the things we do. I know he lives inside a Christian's heart and soul. I touch the center of his Good News every Easter morning. But, honestly, I do not know where he is or why he waits so long,

I am always on the lookout for him; waiting and watching. Every time a fellow soul comes by, every time I look into another's eyes, every time the door opens to the street, at every turning of the road, on every street corner, at the crest of every hill, I am looking for him. I know what this belief can and does do for all our lower moments. But, oh, it takes a long, long time. Spring does not come in a day. The earth is unbelievably old; mankind was long in coming; the world God wants is not yet here. Since Eden is gone, and heaven is not yet here, we live on, as Tillich said, "between the times."

In Paul's listing of the sins of men and women, he does not miss a single one: "fornication, impurity, licentiousness, idolatry, sorcery, enmity, strife, jealousy, anger, selfishness, dissension, party spirit, envy, drunkenness, carousing, and the like" (Galatians 5: 19-21). Any and all of them were present with those whose lives are recorded in the Scriptures, and any and all of them (except perhaps sorcery) are present in our lives today.

Adam and Eve's disobedience and refusal to listen to the Lord God, whether Eden was an actual historical garden or not, does not matter. It is not unlike the self-centered decision-making we see around us now. Kings Saul, David and Solomon were as strong, or as weak, as our leaders are today. A glance at the 12 Disciples reveals a similar pattern of behavior that is seen in the people of the churches across our land.

It takes a long, long time for spring to come and stay in matters of human dignity. Yet I sense a movement there; perhaps I just imagine it. I see people rising again after life has knocked them down. That takes a long, long time. As my old friend Bill said, "When I think how far we have yet to go, I get discouraged. But when I think how far we have come, I get the courage to go on."

Sometimes I see a weakening in the web of human hatred. I see a thinning in the dark clouds behind which the beauty of the heavens dwells. I see green buds peeking out on naked branches where leaves were never seen before. I notice bigger chinks in the armor of injustice. I see life blossoming in the deepest deserts of the world. I see miracles in medical and surgical treatments almost every day. Prompted by the love of Christ and powered by his Resurrection morning, I see people more concerned with human rights. I see springtime coming closer. When I think how far we have come, I get the courage to go on.

Sometimes it is difficult to see it. No preacher I have ever met is protected from feelings of despair. We keep saying that good triumphs over evil, and that God is working out His purpose, but saying is not always believing.

A man once came to tell me that the mother of his children had died that morning. "What kind of God is this?" he asked me. "Our prayers did not help at all. I believe in Christ, and I prayed for her healing, but she died anyway. Now, I drink myself to sleep at night."

They say that the third day will always come, but where is it in the Middle East? When will it come to ease the problems of my aching heart, or my life, my marriage, my job, or the ghettoes of New Orleans? Oh, it takes a long, long time. If life has forced you down those sad and scary paths, my friend, you need an Easter morning.

The words in Colossians that introduced this chapter belong right here. St. Paul was addressing those who wrestled with the ultimate meaning of life, the question of how the universe was connected to the truth of Christ. "He is the image of the invisible God, the first-born of all creation; for in Him all things were created, in heaven and on earth, visible and invisible, whether thrones or dominions or principalities or authorities – all things were created through Him and for Him."

What Paul means is that the universe, with all its glories and endless movement, reflects the meaning and the purpose that God intended the day the world was made. The universe is not self-contained. It does not contain God within it, but rather God contains it; his providence controls it. The potential for every movement was in the mind of God on Creation Day. All things were created by him and for him, and the universe belongs to Christ. The opening words of the Gospel of John tell us that Jesus, the second person of the Trinity, was there from the foundation of the world.

All things were created for that first Easter morning. It was the moment mankind had waited for, when the last enemy— death—would be defeated. It was the eternal moment; and it is the moment you, too, have been waiting for. But curiously, it is a moment we keep running away from. "There are two great days in your life, two irreplaceable and eternally meaning- ful days," wrote Professor William Barclay. "There is the day that you are born, and there is the day that you discover why."

There was a cross planted in the heart of God long before one was planted on Calvary hill outside Jerusalem. Theologian Emil Bruner once stated that the atonement cannot be con- fined to a single occurrence 2000 years ago: it must be remem- bered often in the lives we live today. We need to have a re-cre- ation every time Easter comes, and make every moment poten- tially an Easter moment.

Henrik Isben told the story of the Emperor Julian and his struggle with the Christian faith. The Emperor dreamed of a world where Jesus' name would be eliminated from the earth. He wanted all the commotion caused by Christianity to go away. One night Julian dreamed of a world in which his wish had been granted. The name of Jesus had been removed, just as some critics say it should be in America. The Emperor stood crowned with glory, grateful that this weak and suffering Christ had been erased from time.

But as he stood on the top of the hill, he spied a slow procession of people coming up behind him from way down the hill—soldiers, judges, priests and executioners—and in the middle of them, tired, stooped, and stumbling on, was the one he called "that crazy Galilean," carrying a cross on his shoulder. The Emperor Julian demanded to know what was going on, since Jesus had been eliminated from the earth. "Who is this?," he demanded. "What is this procession?" "We are a procession up to Golgotha to cure the sins of the world," the Galilean replied. He keeps coming back again. He will never go away, ever.

Julian missed it. You could miss it, too. You can wander up to the top of any homemade hill you have, you can try to run away from yourself, but everywhere you go, every time you turn around, in the hour of your departure you will see that proud procession going up the Via Dolorosa, and the same Galilean will be staring at you, carrying a cross on his shoulder.

A little girl in Vermont awakened one early spring day. The snow was gone, the grass was green again, a touch of color was at the edge of the garden and bright yellow forsythia was blooming outside her window. She bounded into her grandparents' room saying, "Wake up, everybody, wake up! The world is beginning again!"

I offer that little story as a precious gift. Spring has sprung, brought to you not so much by the location of the spinning earth in its orbit, but rather arriving from within the longing of your soul, from the little voice that urges you to step into the realm where logic does not matter quite so much and feast on the power and peace of Resurrection morning.

It is time to catch it now, for spring goes by as quickly as it comes. I, too, blinked my eyes one April, and I missed it. It goes back and forth, changing places with the cold of winter and the heat of summer. Catch it while you can, and hold on to it. The earth withers, the flowers fade, but the Risen Christ is here for now and forever more. Amen.

VIII

THE TRANSFORMATION OF AN "IF"

"If Christ is not raised, your faith is in vain."
1 CORINTHIANS. 15:14

I think I saw it in a book by Halford Luccock some years ago, a copy of a Saturday Review cartoon that was a parody on the well-known ancient Greek messenger, who ran 26 miles to tell his people that the Greeks had conquered the Persian army at Marathon. To this day, a 26-mile run is called a marathon. If you recall your history (or legend), you will remember that it took every last ounce of his energy. When he arrived, he had just enough left to whisper, "Victory," before falling exhausted in a dead heap.

The cartoon was a different version, naturally. It pictured the same group of Athenians waiting anxiously for the news, but at the end they were rewarded by a little runner with spindly legs and sagging body, who raced all the way and stumbled to the finish only to say, "Oh darn, I forgot the message." Twenty-six miles of steady running to get to his great moment, and he forgot what he was supposed to say.

Funny, isn't it? It portrays the kind of difficulties you and I face as we seek to celebrate Easter and respond to the

Resurrection. A lot of people have run hard to bring us to this place. Say nothing here of the Church staff and secretaries and volunteers and administrators who ran hard this past week. Say nothing of the other ministers on our staff who do not get to do the preaching, but keep the Church fires burning. Add a word for the altar committee who ran around preparing this sanctuary with beautiful lilies for this morning. Tack on a brief word for those of you who drove or flew across the country to be with your families and who have come to hear the Good News of the Gospel. Don't forget the mothers who ran around the house to get their children here on time. And please do not forget the choirs, who have rehearsed hard to lead us all in worship. It took a lot of running so that we could spend this hour together.

And what should we say, now that we are here? Will we shout the single word, "Victory," or whimper the cartoon version, "Oh, darn, I forgot the message." There are some of you, no doubt, on both sides. Livingston once said that life promises more than it delivers. And we promise more than Christianity delivers if we pretend that all the problems in the world and in our lives will go away because it's Easter. They won't. Check the news tomorrow morning and you will see that no matter what the Christian Church proclaims today, the world will be the same.

I sometimes think it is really worse than the daily papers say. "Oh, it's getting bad," the critics say. "We had better do this or that before it is too late. Time is running out. The Atomic Doomsday clock is ticking, and it is already just a couple of minutes before the midnight hour. If pollution doesn't get us, overpopulation will, or despair, or the bomb, or an earthquake, or war, or wind, or the Middle East cauldron, or fire, or famine, or peril, or sword." <u>Scientific American</u> magazine reminded me the other day that the sun continues to burn itself out; it has only approximately 200 million years to go, give or take a few. It is an age of worry and upheaval. Do you want to hear a positive Easter message in your corner of the world?

Let's look at the original story. The runner arrived exhausted by the journey, but he knew the right word: victory. The battle is over, and Christ is victorious. Paul jumps in there in I Corinthians 15, only 50 miles away from Athens and 2000 years from you and me, to tell you what it means to him: one word in Christ—"Victory." That's the news. It's not that Paul was naïve and unrealistic. He could match any one of us in the depths of personal worry and fear. He finally gave his life for the cause of Christ and his people, but the last word is the first: "Victory!"

I will never forget the little girl who's Southeastern Division of the intermediate slow pitch softball team had just won the Third Subdivision championship. It was a hectic last inning. The girls really got into the game, cheered on mainly by their parents and grandparents. No World Series game ever had more enthusiastic fans. I think the final score was 18 to 16. Anyway, when the final out was posted, the winning team came running in from the field to the applause and cheers of their fans. But the tiny right fielder was not aware of what had happened. She has been biding her time counting the daisies in her corner of the field. So, when the game ended, she smiled broadly and asked, "Hey Coach John, did we win?" How funny! She was the victor, and she did not even know it. But it's not as funny as those who have an Easter morning victory and do not know it either!

It is not what you look at, said Thoreau, it is what you see. It is not what is happening, but what you make of it. Always, there are two dynamics at work: the present and the future are running side-by-side and neck-to-neck. The same bugle sounds the taps as sounds the reveille. The same piper calls the troops to battle as pipes a highland fling. The same drum sounds the muffled beat at graveside as rolls with the raising of the flag. The end and the beginning are two parts of the same movement.

Look at the chaos of our world and cry over it, or try to see the beginning of a new and better world. Breaking down the walls that separate us from each other is hard and thankless work. It makes a lot of noise and dirt; people's backs break and ache. See the walls and the dust, or see the broadening in human worth and dignity. I still like the construction sign that says, "Temporary inconvenience, but permanent improvement." Look at the apparent disintegration of organized religion and the decline of influence of the Christian Church, or try to see a resurrection of a deeper and more honest faith among the young. In this Easter season, I sense a movement toward a lovelier day. I hear people facing problems honestly, and I see them making it, as well.

In some ways, when you think about the plethora of problems, it reminds me of the British Sea Captain who once announced with typical British reserve to the passengers and crew of his ship as it struggled through the roughest sea: "Ladies and Gentlemen, I am here to assure you that everything will be all right, provided the ship doesn't split down the middle." Nobody laughed.

All of us must muster that kind of courage for the living of these days. The ship itself is in the hands of God; if it cracks down the middle, there isn't much we can do about it. But as long as we are here, let us celebrate the life Christ gave us. Michael Quoist wrote, "Many people say that everything is falling apart, and the world itself is passing away. But I say a new world is being born." And so do I. A world where the purposes of God will work their way in time, and he will work his plan. You can be sure of that, or you cannot be sure of anything at all.

That's the message, or part of it and that brings us back to Paul, where he is making a case for the resurrection of the Christ. "Now, I would remind you brothers, in what terms I preached to you the gospel, which you received, in which you stand, by which you are saved, if you hold fast, unless you believed in vain. I delivered to you as of first importance what I also received, that Christ was raised on the third day in accordance with the Scriptures. . . But if there is no resurrection, then we are found to be misrepresenting God, your faith is in vain, and of all men we are to be most pitied." (1 Corinthians 15, selected verses)

It is all right there, to be understood and believed. We make a mistake when we assume that only modern men doubt the miracles of the Scripture, as if all earlier men were dupes to any fantastic story that the ancient world conjured up, as if they did not know what inconsistency was or what a contradiction sounded like. We are not superior. They were not dumb. They had questions, too. Paul was presenting his case to counteract those who said it couldn't be true, that life is life, and death is death and when it is over, it's over.

The truth of the matter is that the prevailing attitude of the time was probably no more or less amenable to believing that the Easter stories were true than ours is. Doubt is not a 20th

Century exclusive. Convincing people that a man had come back from the dead was as difficult then as it is now. But Paul does not chide them or ridicule them or toss them out of the sanctuary. He forms a very careful argument. Believe what you will, he writes, but there are consequences. If it is all a hoax, then Christ has played a trick on you, and I do not think a kind and caring loving God would play a trick like that on his children. The One who knows our needs and fears, the One who rules this life and beyond and whose promises are true has not, will not, cannot let us down.

There are three ways to divide Paul's argument. I call this the transformation of an "if."

I. In the first place, I like the matter-of-fact way that Paul gets to the heart of the question. Believe what you will—it is your choice—but if Christ is not raised, then the wrong side has won. The nails and spears and two big sticks of wood and the hot Palestinian sun have won the battle. There is no other choice. Either God was victorious, or indecisive, fearful, manipulative Pontius Pilate took the day. That's it. When you roll up your sleeves and dive into the middle of what Easter is all about, there is one choice and no alternative.

Either the Prince of Peace was victorious, or sneaky old Herod and cautious Caiaphas wear the crowns. You can pick your side. Either it was the supreme hour of all history, and we hold fast to it, or we toss up our hands and fall dead in an exhausted heap with no message to remember beyond what we can see and touch and feel. Then Jesus becomes the good guy with a good life lived under trying circumstances with good grace. But when the mechanism that keeps your life and mine alive is interrupted, that's all there is. Over and out.

Believe what you will, but your alternative is that the battle is lost, and Paul pities you. Christ tells you at Easter that life and death are not opposites, but they are two parts to the same story. In the end, life endures. Pascal once said that the risk in believing was the better choice to make. You can bet your life on it. Either our lives are in the hands of God for now and forever more, or life loses every time death intervenes. That's what Paul was saying: if Christ is not raised, your faith is in vain. If you can choose between life and death, choose life!

II. Secondly, some of you might still want to suspend judgment on the Resurrection miracle itself. Still we can move Paul's sentence to a broader meaning and deeper level beyond resurrection from the dead. Paul could be saying, "If the message of Christianity is not true, then human life itself is also lived in vain." There is a difference. John Baillie, the eminent Scottish theologian of the mid-20th Century, once said, "The theologian should never say 'only,' he should always say, 'at least.'" Never place a period where God has placed a comma. Never end the paragraph when there is more to say. We should never say that Christianity is "only" for those who are able to accept all the details of the faith. It also applies to those who have reservations. The emphasis in the Pauline Epistles, as in the Gospels, is not so much on the human form that rose from the dead: the Greek verb is passive – he was raised. It might seem a trifle picayune, but Jesus did not raise himself up out of the tomb; God raised him.

The early Church did not believe so much in the Resurrection because they found an empty tomb, but because they found the spirit of the living Christ alive. Their emphasis was on what God could do, not "only" on what he had done.

There is always more to come. The ultimate question was not whether Jesus escaped the tomb and flew up into the sky, but whether God vindicated the one who was rejected by men. Here, again, there is only one choice to make: either the insight of our faith that proclaims a God who cares for us is true—either we see the love God has for us in the life of Jesus—or we know nothing beyond the boundaries of the here and now. That's not a very good choice.

The mission and ministry of Jesus were victorious. "The days of our years are three score and ten, and if by strength they be four score, yet is their span labor and sorrow. They are soon gone and we fly away." (Psalm 90) Is that where you would rest your case? Not that we should pretend perfection and ease. Anxiety is inevitable in an age of crises. But do not make it worse by deceiving yourself. There is a time to be anxious. Someone once parodied Kipling's famous lines to read, "If you can keep your head when all about you are losing theirs and blaming it on you, then perhaps you don't really know what's going on."

At a gathering I attended in England's Oxford Union, a famous Clergyman was asked by a rambunctious young student if life was worth living. The Archbishop thought a few seconds before replying, "I think it is, but what on earth else are you going to do with it?" There is no other choice except to end it—none at all. Either you live life in the confidence that our times are in the hands of God and that the whole life process is heading toward a destination already chosen, or you are left with the stark fact of nonexistence without meaning. Life is toil and trouble, then we fly away and there's nothing more. Believe what you will about the universe of God and man, but be prepared to accept the consequences of a life where the embodiment of love in Christ is not involved.

III. Third and last, there is a final way to phrase Paul's question: "If the universe itself cannot be trusted, then your faith, hope and life are all in vain." Again, there is a single choice. This section is for those of you who say honestly, "You could be right, but from what I see, it does not fit. Christianity is just one of the many religions that talks about the gods who came to earth. The Easter story is nothing but a reenactment of the spring resurrection myths from the ancient world."

If that's your thing, there is an "if" for you as well. Beyond talk of God and Christ and resurrection, there remains the question of what to make of life and of the universe itself. Schiller said that life is aimless, that man is worthless, just a self-aggrandizing part of matter stuck on his own importance: "Man is muck, makes muck, and will return to muck." But Schiller is wrong again, as are all the rest who prattle on that way. I choose the opposite view. As Robert Frost once said, "In all the uncertainty, there is a still enough to go ahead with." We can go ahead with our transformation, if you can at least claim this much as your own. I would ask for more, but admit at least the universe is compatible with our highest hopes. If you cannot get that far, then there is nowhere else to go.

I am always stunned by Franz Kafka's short story, <u>The Hunger Artist,</u> about a pathetic creature in a circus sideshow who went on a hunger strike. That was his talent – he knew how to keep from eating food. They put him in a cage along the way up to the center tent. Day after day as he wasted away, people came to stare at him and marvel at how long a man could last without tasting any food. Great spectacle! It was sad to see.

But it ends in a Kafka-sequel kind of twist. A reporter comes up to the cage and asks him why he is doing it. "Why do you go on fasting; your life will be in danger, why do you do it?" the reporter asks. The creature whispers back—and nothing can erase the horror of his final words: "I couldn't find the food I liked." How pathetic. I could not find the food I liked, so I starved myself to death.

And you will starve, too, if you try to swallow a universe that cannot be trusted and that is alien to the highest hopes you have. Nothing will erase the horror of those final words when you are terribly alone, wandering endlessly through the caverns of your own making. Believe what you will—it's your choice, but be prepared to take the consequences. If the universe is hostile or uncaring, then life is all in vain. If it is aimless and out-of-tune with the music of the eternal spheres, then when darkness comes again, when the whole experiment goes dark for good, cacophony and nihilism win the day.

So, let us transform that "if" completely by removing it and replacing it with "since." Since Christ is raised, since Christianity is real, and since the universe is compatible with our highest hopes, then neither your faith, nor your hopes, nor your life, or mine, can ever be in vain.

Don't forget the message. Don't go into your soul or out into the waiting world, both of which are dying for the news, and fall exhausted to the ground whimpering, "Sorry, I forgot the news," or worse, "I never found the message I was looking for." You do not need to ask the coach if your team won the game. Or course they did—Jesus did. Speak it one more time within this service, and say it over and over and over throughout this day and in all the days and decades yet to come. The word is, "Victory"! Let us sing about it now and forever more. Amen.

> *The strife is o'er*
> *The battle done*
> *The victory of life is won*
> *The song of triumph has begun.*
> *Alleluia. Amen.*

IX

MORNING HAS BROKEN

"Now on the first day of the week they came to the tomb early,
while it was still dark,
and saw that the stone had been rolled away.
They were perplexed, and the angels said
to them, 'Why do you seek the living among the dead?
He is risen, as he said.'"

Luke 24: 1-4

The whole world seeks an Easter morning, and it was no different back in the days and nights when Jesus walked the earth. He had come to bring them abundant life, and because he mastered life where they had failed, they took him to Calvary and finished him for good.

For his friends and followers, the darkness of death lasted for two full nights, three days in total. The Scripture says they rested on the Saturday following the Crucifixion. But what a strange, non-refreshing kind of rest it would have been. No one who has lost someone they loved too much to lose ever manages to arise from such early nights of sleep refreshed and renewed. But, on the third day, the new Christian world poked up through the darkness to see that Christ the Lord had risen from the dead.

To the chosen few, it was a friend—even family—who had died. He had been the single most important living soul in all their lives. He was the source of all their joy. When they wondered what the crazy mixed-up world was all about, they found an answer in him. And for those first few days following his crucifixion, their hearts and heads and hopes could not believe what had happened. Surely this bad dream would pass on, as it always had before, they thought. But Friday noon would become a cruel trick, a bad dream from which there was no waking.

If you have ever walked that road yourself, you know how dazed they felt in the stark loneliness of those first hours. It was all over, and he was gone. Desperate and lonely, afraid and empty, they passed the hours and waited, thinking he would come back through the door any minute, even though they knew deep down that he would not. Time passed slowly.

Little wonder, then, that while it was still dark on Sunday morning, they could wait no longer. Out they went to visit the tomb where two days before they had wept while Joseph of Arimathea and his servants took Jesus' body down from the cross and tenderly buried it in a borrowed tomb. The women watched while a monumental stone was rolled up into the trough to guard the entrance. A lovely spot I think it must have been, quiet, peaceful, a place to let the mind wander over what had been or what might have been, if what happened had not happened.

So before dawn on Sunday, the women went tiptoeing up to the tomb to anoint the body of the one they loved. There is bravery in that alone, just walking in the dark up to a tomb where someone you love is under the earth or behind the stone. The first friend I lost to death was a young girl named Audrey, a teenager who was killed in a car wreck by a drunken driver, long before MADD mothers called it to national attention. I felt it was the right thing to do, so I went alone to her grave in the cemetery. I was not aware that it was getting toward dusk. When I arrived, I found that the earth that had been used to cover over the coffin had sunken in, especially on the corner of the grave nearest to me. It made me so uncomfortable that I hurried away and said a prayer for Audrey when I got back to the gate.

When the women arrived on that first Easter, they must have been feeling some of the same. Spooky is the word we use. They were also wondering how they could roll the huge stone away. But the Scripture says that the stone was already rolled back, and the tomb was empty. What a shock! Luke says they were perplexed, that they could not believe it. Mary, almost frantic with fear, said to someone standing there, "Sir, they have taken away the body of my Friend and Lord. Tell me where they have laid him." That someone was the Lord Jesus himself, but her eyes were so filled with grief and tears that she did not recognize him. He said, "Woman, why are you weeping?" When she looked up, he said simply, "Mary." Hearing his voice, she knew that it was Jesus. She had seen the Lord. She did not realize it at the time, but daybreak had come up over the hillsides of Jerusalem, and the night was over and gone. Morning had broken, and the light was there to stay. What the world needed then, and now, was light. All the sunshine she would ever need was standing there in front of her. It was Life itself in the person of Jesus the Christ.

That's where we begin. Morning breaks in so many other ways; hope is found in many other corners of the universe; life is celebrated here and there and everywhere; but in the Garden outside a borrowed tomb, the light illuminating eternity had opened its Easter eyes. All the other bits and pieces of revelation come second to this single salient moment.

Perhaps you cannot or will not believe it. There are legions outside our stained glass windows who would chide that it is just some artificial balm to soothe the agonies of life, a made-up myth to fit the ancient scene, a kind of opiate to help weaklings through the terrifying darkness of the world.

Some would shout that modern men and women look elsewhere for emotional strength and peace, that the old religions are tired and old. One writer suggested that in 30 years, Christianity would be a memory (that was in 1976). Others will not accept that it comes down to a question of what God wants to make of the here and now, and of you and me, and all the other children of the earth.

Perhaps you are too wedded to the present, giving, getting, shuffling to and fro, and making progress on the road to nowhere or to success. Perhaps you will go away this morning just exactly as you came in. I hope not. What you need is here for the asking. Some of us will not leave empty-handed. Some will see more clearly than they ever have seen before, believing where they cannot prove, trusting where they cannot see, and edging up to the tomb while it is still dark.

I pose a question here for your consideration: if the possibility of life that conquers death is not the first item on your agenda, if the message of eternal victory is not your primary concern, then pray tell me, what is? Would you wed your purpose to the machinations of this life alone? Would you say that men and women find their ultimate significance in battering and being battered? Would you allow that time and chance and accidents and micro-organisms that destroy the body can also destroy the soul? Can the essential stuff of all that God intended be subject to death? What kind of God, I ask you, would it be whose power is so finite? Would you choose to believe that chance is the destiny of man and God's creation? Would you choose a universe that is alien to the highest hopes of men and women? If this is not the message of Easter, what other message could it be?

Ah, well, you are entitled to your personal answer. I have mine. You can choose whatever form you like to bring meaning to the creation. But someone or something brought it here. Someone or something was behind the process when darkness was upon the face of the deep, bringing light and love and life and loveliness.

If you had been there at the moment of creation, if you had heard the sound of that initial explosion, if you had watched that tiny speck of matter flare out to the farthest reaches of the universe, and if someone had tried to assure you that from the horrid din of the opening Big Bang, a new order would eventually arise, and that human life would one day begin, and further those human beings made in the image of God would learn to love and care about each other—you would have shouted defiantly, "No way, no way José. It will never happen." But it did.

In the movement of time and space, the universe fits together. Everything is related to a plan and purpose that emanates from the mind of the Creator. How stupid it would be to say that it just happened, and by choice, chance and misdirection it became the integrated unit that it is. Do you think that molten mass of energy could transform itself into a living, loving, and human being all by itself? That would be as stupid as declaring that your grandfather clock came about when someone shook a bag of wood, glass and metal, tossed them on the floor, and presto, a working clock happened to be made. That image is not to cast our lot with those who believe that the evolution of things was guided by the unseen hand. It is just to say that when you look around the universe, you know it cannot have come by chance. Of course, we cannot know its secrets, but the Bible promises that one day we will: "What is hidden will one day be made known." Meanwhile, we must stumble around to find the missing links; the universe does not reveal its secrets without forcing us to find the building blocks ourselves.

A friend of mine likens the whole process to the familiar Easter Egg Hunts which are practiced in Christian homes, Churches, and even at the White House. In our home through the years, after we had dyed the eggs, with the children helping, we used to hide them the night before Easter. When our daughters were young we chose easy hidey holes. The older they became, the more care we took to find out of the way places. One year the Easter Bunny was so inspired, we never found two of the eggs until the next year when we went to hide a new batch of eggs. We do not recommend that.

Anyway, come Easter morning, or sometimes with our Sunday Schedule, we had to wait until the last Church service was over, so we could all participate as a family. The children searched here and there and everywhere to find the hidden eggs. When they would find one, they giggled and jumped for joy, racing back to their baskets, trying to best each other and find the most eggs. Now and then Mrs. Cromie and I would offer hints about how cold or warm they were in the search, depending on how close we were to the time for dinner or the time to go to visit the Grandparents.

My friend said that he often feels the Easter Egg search reminds him of the way God deals with his children. A little egg is hidden here and another there, some more obvious than others, making it more intricate the deeper we plod on. The Bible often refers to the God who hides from his people. In the

Psalms especially, reference is made to the hidden God. (Psalm 10,13,51,89 and 119). The New Testament mentions how in Jesus Christ the hidden God is revealed. Colossians Two says that "all the treasures and wisdom" are hidden in Christ. St. Paul in Romans 1 reminds us that what can be known of the Creator is plain; but still it is a difficult to fathom the depths of all that is there. As a thoughtful parent, God hides the "eggs", as it were, and then shows us little hints to make our guesses work. At least he does not abandon us to the search on our own.

Someone or something lies behind it all, or it would not and could not be. If you can rest your case with an entity that could not care less about your life, choose it if you will, but I warn you, you will be stuck with it. You must live then without hope and believe that the existentialists are correct when they say, "Life begins in pain, prolongs itself in weakness and in fear, and then it dies by chance."

The choice to believe is not all that unreasonable and childish. It is not all that primitive and mythological. Authentication of life and death lies beyond the touch of scientific realism in the realm of faith and good theology. If man's chief glory is to think, then think on.

The Easter morning message is not alien to the way we think and feel in all the other stations and places of our lives. Do not get lost in the labyrinth of what you conclude about the miracle itself. The One who has the power to create a universe can surely guard your individual life. The One who made the world out of nothing can surely remake a spiritual body from the ravages of death. Surely! Yet some remain reluctant to commit to it themselves.

When Arthur Compton won the Nobel Prize in Physics, he confessed, "Every discovery I ever made, I gambled that the truth was there, and then I acted on the gamble in faith until I could prove that it was true." Often, if not always, we believe things first and then prove them later on. We feel our love and loveliness and then we test it. We sense beauty and then we confirm it. We all live on the hope that what we dream about and need will one day be supplied. The whole world needs an Easter. The whole world needs to know that life is more than we see ending every day. The whole world needs to know that you and I and every other living, breathing soul that is or was or ever will be are rooted in some grand eternal purpose beyond the whim of time and change and chance.

That's what gives credence to the dignity of individuals. If we are not made in the image of God and belong to the natural lifeline of the animal kingdom, the sanctity of each living soul disappears completely. That is why we care for ourselves and for each other. If man is just a thing, here today and gone tomorrow, it really does not matter what we do to ourselves or to anyone else. If there is no worth to life, then those who treat human beings as expendable are justified. Hitler tried to sort them out, to keep the good and "perfect" ones, and throw away the rest. He failed. It took a lot of time and courage and fallen lives to bring his downfall. But if life has no more purpose than being puppets to those who take the reins, then Adolph Hitler and Joseph Stalin win the day.

If God does not care, then why should we? Weak, so-judged "imperfect" human beings can be driven into the fires of Treblinka, Stalin's Gulag, or into the cotton fields and factories back home without reprobation or recompense. Unless there is something significant and everlasting about what they are, unless we are made in the image of God, what other motivation do we have to treat all men, women and children as precious and equal? What other motivation is there to tolerate those who disrupt our progress? What other way is there to jus-

102

tify the energy and time we use to care, weep and pray for the poor wrecks of humankind? The answer is that without the gift of holiness, without being made in the image and for the purposes of God, without being part of His creation, people would be problems, never persons.

This is what Easter morning means: human beings belong to much more than death. The Creator of the universe cares for us beyond what we do in the years we live. Think about it: Easter reassures us that life is safe in the hands of the One who formed us from the earth itself. The one who made the starry heavens knows you and me by name.

We live our days on this round ball of matter whirling about in a universe so big we cannot see or comprehend how far and fast it is expanding. We live where the streams meander around the valleys, where green grass grows, where cherry trees blossom, and where life and loveliness abound. But we also live where floods come, hurricanes howl, tornadoes blow life away, rock slides and lava flows crush and cover all we make and are, and people hate and kill each other. We live in a precarious balance of a solar system that could fly off the handle any second and send us hurling through space, and on an earth that could blow itself to smithereens at any time.

But Easter takes us higher. Easter morning gives us the larger picture. A stone was rolled in to guard the tomb, just as huge stones are often rolled across our path to block our passageway. But the women came and found the stone was no longer there. If you have to walk through the valley, it helps to have someone hold your hand, and the Risen Christ was standing there to do it.

There are days when it is dark, days when the storms gather such momentum and force that even the strongest of us bows in fear. There are times when our path is blocked, and we do not know what to do. Robert Frost told about the day a lightning storm dropped a huge oak tree over the driveway up to his farmhouse in Vermont. But in time, lumber men cut it up and carried the wood to his farmhouse to warm it in winter. It was a huge obstacle, but a removable one. If you catch the gist of Easter morning, you have an image of what is happening to the obstacle called death.

You need an Easter morning. You need a rebirth of your individual spirit. You need to see yourself standing there in disbelieving awe. If God loves you, you need to believe in your own worth. Christ believes in you. He thinks that you are something special. The Creator God loved you and me so much that he sent his only Son to die that we might live a full life here and continue to live it into eternity. You are a child of God; you are related to the King of all the universe.

We all need an Easter morning! Each of us needs to have our stones rolled away. Are you worried that your son or daughter will disappoint themselves, or you? You need an Easter morning. Are you worried for your loneliness, wondering how you will ever find the joy of life again? Are you growing older, not so gracefully and now concerned about your future? Does the illness that has struck your loved one tear your heart and hopes away? You need an Easter morning. You need to stand back and let the love of God roll away whatever stone is blocking your path. You need to let the power of God break in on your life. You need to stand back and turn it all over to the One who controls your life and the lives of those you love. You need to know that the One who made you and claimed you is able to keep you.

I had a book by Martin Gray called, For Those I Loved. It is the touching story of a young Polish lad who got caught in the ugly trap the Nazis set for the Jews of Europe. He ran with the rejects of the underground. He was arrested and incarcerated in a concentration camp where thousands died. He was forced to work on the death squad when his wife and family were executed. Finally, he escaped.

Twenty years after all the agony, his new wife and their four children perished in an enormous forest fire in Southern France. Crushed and alone again, he formed a foundation to help little children without parents in all parts of the world. He wrote, "I am living, doing things, keeping active. I escaped Treblinka. I survived. I built my fortress. But all fortresses are frail, temporary. I am still on the move. I don't want to live for myself. . . . I'm still living for my people, living in and through them. I'm remembering that there are a host of unknown people, my immemorial people, to whom I'm accountable for my actions. I confuse all the faces. I'm nothing except what they made me. . . Alone I'm nothing. I live for those I loved, and for those who once loved me." What a story! What a hero! What a Christian!

Henry Francis Lytle was a Scottish Anglican minister in the early 19th Century, who developed an enormous church program in Devon. Far ahead of his time, he had a Christian education schedule with 800 regular students. He trained 70 teachers a year himself, and he always had a team of substitutes ready to back the regulars up in times of illness. He called on the members of his parish. He wrote books about theology. He even directed the music program of the church and wrote hymns. Little wonder that his health gave out, and he left the ministry far ahead of the normal retirement age.

On his last Sunday at the Brixham Church, he walked into the garden and got so involved in the moment that he wrote the magnificent hymn, Abide With Me, in only a few minutes. It reflects his own weariness, his failing health and waning spirit, his problems and his loneliness, his sense of the approaching end. It is in the last stanza that he found his strength:

Hold thou Thy cross before my closing eyes,
Shine through the gloom and point me to the skies,
Heaven's morning breaks and earth's vain shadows flee,
In life, in death, O Lord, abide with me.

I titled this chapter Morning Has Broken. The popular singer Cat Stevens modernized an old folk song, which serves as the background of our Easter message:

Morning has broken like the first morning,
Blackbird has spoken like the first bird.
Praise for the singing! Praise for the morning!
Praise for them springing fresh from the Word!

Sweet the rain's new fall sunlit from heaven,
Like the first dewfall on the first grass.
Praise for the sweetness of the wet garden,
Sprung into completeness where His feet pass.

Mine is the sunlight! Mine is the morning
Born of the one light Eden saw play!
Praise with elation, praise every morning,
God's recreation of the new day!

I hope you experience God's RE-creation of the new day, as a new Easter morning breaks now and forevermore. Amen.

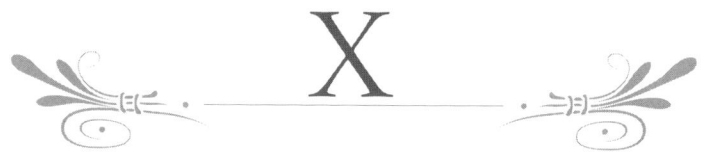

X

EASTER MORNING AT THE MALL
So What Else is New This Spring?

A story and a sermon based on Matthew 28: 1-10

The Story

Many years ago I revived an old Easter tradition by opening my Easter sermon with a story. The story stood on its own,
unrelated to the sermon. Its only purpose was to make the congregation laugh. These Easter tales were always enthusiastic,
even a trifle outrageous at times. Some other preachers I know
who have come across my published sermons, have borrowed
my custom, and in a few cases, they stole my story.

My rational for this peculiar behavior came from my
research into the misty past of the medieval Christian church,
back when the Lenten Fast of 40 days was a fast indeed. To
please the Lord, and to punish themselves, Christians gave up
practically everything that brought them pleasure. It was a
struggle.

Well, you can imagine what great relief it was when Lent
was finally over. We have little idea of that seasonal joy today,
for we hardly give up anything at all for Lent. My father, the
son of an Ulster Scot from Ballygorian, County Down, taught
me that God did not require us to "give up" anything. We were

to "take up" a new spiritual discipline. I must confess that one can easily duck that advice and give up and take up nothing.

But not back then. When Lent was finally over, and it was time for the 6:00 a.m. mass on Easter morning, the people and the priests were exhausted, having celebrated all night—to say little of their states of equilibrium.

You can just imagine how the Reverend Fathers—for the most part good, religious men—could have slipped into the same condition by the time the Easter services began (after all, priests and pastors are human). They, too, took up what they had given up. Feeling excited and pleasantly relaxed, they began to entertain their large congregations with humorous, even slightly off-color and later on, absolutely ribald stories.

Thus began what is officially called a *Risus Pachalis,* which in Latin means "an Easter joke." As the stories became more and more ridiculous, Pope Clement X, the old spoil-sport that he was, finally issued a Papal decree outlawing jokes from the pulpit at Easter Sunday Mass. This all is true and historically verifiable.

To prove I am a Calvinist and unfazed by papal decrees, I intend to tell you a *Risus Pachalis.* (You might wish you had gone to St. Edward's Roman Catholic Church by the time I have finished my story.) This *Risus Pachalis* is an old story, but a still meaningful one about persistence in prayer.

You see there was this proper Presbyterian woman who had a perky little parrot as a pet, and the parrot's name was Polly. A nicer parrot you would never want to see, prim and proper and pretty. The only problem was that Polly had an awful habit. Whenever she met anyone new she screeched out loud, as parrots can, "Whoopee, Charlie, I'm a good time girl!"

One fine day the woman's pastor came to call. And sure

enough, you guessed it, Polly let out with one of her famous, "Whoopie, Charlie, I'm a good time girl!" yells. Oh, the Reverend sure was shocked, to say nothing of the proper owner of the parrot.

"I'm so sorry," she said. "Don't worry about it, dear. I think that I can help you," said the reverend. "You see, I have two parrots down in my study at the Church. They are very well behaved indeed, and I think they would be a good influence on your Polly. In fact, all they ever do all day long is pray.

So, the Reverend took the misbehaving Polly to Church. When he entered his lovely study with Polly in tow, sure enough his own two parrots were respectfully praying, bowed down low on their little swings in their cage. Seeing them, Polly Parrot was ecstatic. Immediately she bellowed out her, "Whoopee, Charlie, I'm a good time girl!" upon which the parson's proper parrots stirred. One opened his right eye and cocked his head to see. Then, with one of his wings, he nudged the other parrot gently and cackled quite excitedly: "Hey Luke, you better wake up. I think we finally got what we've been praying for!"

The Sermon

Years ago, while on my way to attend an Easter Sunrise sermon at a Pittsburgh Mall, I received a Paschal inspiration, just by looking in the mall windows. You dare not plan an outdoor Easter Sunrise Service in Pittsburgh because it is often too cold. I was a little late, and as I entered on the second floor of the mall, I could hear the hymn, "Jesus Christ is Risen Today" rising up from the ground floor below. Easter was in the air. I saw people in fine new dresses, dozens of colorful balloons in a net waiting to be released, a brass ensemble, and a huge ecumenical choir. The Reverend clergy were adorned in rich sartorial splendor. What a sight and what a sound!

I looked around. Always on the watch for potential sermon topics, I noticed a sermon staring back at me. Inside the shop windows were dozens of finely adorned mannequins within ear-shot of the Easter songs and message, but they could not have cared less. They remained entirely still, unmoved and unphased. A few of the mannequins were males, but not a one was in the least concerned with Easter. I concluded that the mannequins were like some people of the church who dress up in Easter finery, looking grand and nice and new, but hang around the fringes unmoved and unmoving. Ho hum, another Easter.

It reminded me of what I once read about Christopher Wren's famous St. Paul's Cathedral in London. Because of its weight and the unsettled land beneath it, the Cathedral moves down Fleet Street about a quarter of an inch per century. I do not mean to be judgmental, but in the comparison between the mannequins and the real live Christians and how slowly they sometimes move, I noted a similarity to the movement forward of the famous Cathedral, inching along imperceptibly.

If you had been there at the first Easter Sunrise, minding your own matters, nursing your private emotional needs on the third day after your whole world caved in, you might have noticed how few people were enthused by the Resurrection. Then around 8:00 a.m. a little group of women came rushing in, chattering on about how they could not find the body when they had come to the tomb before dawn. You can't blame the Disciples who refused to believe the Easter story when they first heard it. "These words seemed to them an idle tale, and they did not believe them," Luke says.

"Oh come on now, settle down", you might say. "Grief is a potent enemy. It can make you kind of crazy. It steals your perspective. It makes you feel and hear and see all kinds of things and wonder, 'Are you sure it wasn't a dream?'"

You shouldn't blame that wee band of brothers. They were sure that if Jesus had decided to come back from the grave to see someone, he would have come to see one of them, not some women.

Yet, I think someone there still wondered what those women really did see. "Nah, it couldn't be. I saw the soldiers take him down and bury him. He was dead, and dead men do not get up and walk away." They didn't know what to think or say.

If you came here this morning not knowing what to believe, at least you are in good company, since the Disciples did not know what to believe, either. If you are one of those who stand by idly, like mannequins at the Mall, and wonder how a sensible preacher could ever believe in the resurrection of Jesus Christ, you need to get your soul and psyche up and have a look for yourself.

Even Socrates back in the pre-Christian era advised his followers to believe in the afterlife. "What do you have to lose? If there is nothing beyond, you will go to sleep forevermore," he said as he swallowed the poison hemlock. That's not all bad if you think about it. "But if there is an afterlife", he added, "you have prepared your way to go there."

To some people, Jesus was a good guy who lived a good life under trying circumstances, to be sure. The crescendo picks up when you think of life and death. Christ tells you on Easter that life and death are not opposites, but are two parts to the same story. In the end, the individual life endures. Either our lives are in the hands of God, or they are not. If not, then life loses each time death comes along. If Christ is not raised, our faith is in vain.

In his great book, <u>Easter Gospels</u>, Dr. Robert H. Smith comments on how honestly Luke faced the same dilemma. Everyone around him, friend and foe alike, had trouble believing that a dead man was alive again. It ran counter to their beliefs. Luke wrote about the Easter story and its aftermath with great care. Dr. Smith says, "Resurrection for them was not easily achieved or lightly held. It rests on something far more substantial than emotions, visions and mere hearsay." Luke tells us that belief arose despite the natural inclination of those who were there to doubt the initial reports. The men on the road to Emmaus in Luke 24 reveal the same. Smith writes that, "The resurrected Christ was forced on them by the evidence!" They had to find room in their minds and souls for a new category of things to incorporate.

One thing is positively certain: those Disciples and family members and earliest followers of Jesus got up and got going. They attached themselves to Jesus and spread the good news. We are assured that we need not fear, or even be ultimately disappointed, by the world that God has made. If the universe itself cannot be trusted, then our faith, hope and lives are all in vain. Professor Karl Barth used to say that the only way to discover what happened is to immerse yourself in the Scriptures. It does not matter how you view the words—just keep reading, and you will see.

If you think the universe is hostile or uncaring, if you end up believing that it is not conducive to all you long to be, then everything you are and hope to be comes into question. If you refuse to get up and go over to the tomb to see what is going on, you might as well be a mannequin in a Mall window, unmoving, unaffected, deaf, dumb, blind, believing nothing, and remaining lifeless, for now and forever more. Amen.

XI

THE MEMORY OF HIS WORDS...

"And they remembered his words, and returning from the Tomb they told all this to the eleven and to all the rest."
LUKE 24:8-9

The women were devastated, of course. Who wouldn't be? Their best friend, their favorite teacher, their beloved pastor, the one they needed more than anyone else in the entire world, was gone. Worse, his passing was gruesome; his final hours devastating and disheartening. His captors flogged him and made fun of him and insulted him with the charade of an illegal trial. When they had had their fill, and Pontius Pilate had showed his true colors, Jesus's once-adoring crowd screamed for his crucifixion. They marched him up the Via Dolorosa to a place outside the town called Golgotha. There, they nailed him to an old wooden cross, hoisted it up, and there he hung in the hot desert sun for hours. The passers-by mocked him and taunted him. They offered him vinegar to drink on a sponge and someone spit at him. The soldiers also scoffed him, babbling, "You saved others, but you cannot save yourself! If you are the Messiah, hop down." How I wish he had.

Finally, this holy, wonderful and innocent man began to

drift in and out of consciousness. They pierced his side with a spear to hasten his death and waited impatiently for him to die. Mercifully, at the ninth hour (about 3:00 in the afternoon), he breathed his last, and cried out, "It is finished." He meant, "It has just begun". And with that he crossed over to the other side.

It was awful. The men, even his closest confidants and Disciples, were so afraid, the Bible says, that they forsook him and fled. But Luke adds, perhaps to show where true courage was that day, "The women who had come with him from Galilee followed, and they saw the Tomb where he was laid by Joseph of Arimathea." Perhaps it was safer and easier for women to be around. As was customary, they returned to their borrowed lodgings where they wept, for sure, and began to prepare spices and ointments to embalm the body of the Lord. Then came the Sabbath (Saturday). They rested on that day, as was required by Jewish law, for they all were Jews. On the first day of the week (our Sunday), at last they could do something.

Sorrow and loss make light sleepers, as you know. They were most likely awake all night; and sometime before the sun came up, they arose and anxiously made their way out to the tomb in Joseph's garden. There, "they found that the stone was rolled away from the tomb," and worse, "when they went into the sepulcher, they did not find the body of the Lord." What on earth was going on? "They were perplexed," Luke wrote. Perplexed indeed!

But perplexity was soon replaced by fear. As they bowed their faces to the ground, "Two men dressed in dazzling white apparel" spoke to them saying, "Why do you seek the living among the dead? He is not here. Remember how he told you in Galilee that he would be delivered into the hands of evil men and be crucified, but that on the third day he would rise again from the dead? Remember? Of course you do...."

Next it says, "They remembered his words, and returning from the Tomb they told all that had happened and what they had heard, first to the 11 Disciples (number 12, Judas Iscariot, had killed himself from guilt that he had betrayed his savior for 30 shekels of silver) "then they told it to all the rest." It does not say who "the rest" were, but it seems that the mother of Jesus was there, and perhaps a couple of his brothers and sisters comforting her, and some devoted friends from Galilee, and the group of women who followed him and cared for him throughout his three years of ministry.

But when the women told them what they had seen and heard, nobody believed them, not a one, none, nada. To the apostles, their words seemed to be an idle tale. No one believed them! There have been many others since who do not believe them either, with far less to go on.

There are two ways to look at the Gospel records that describe the first Easter morning. One is from a purely historical viewpoint. It has been the mainstay of believers for 1900 years: "Just read it and believe it." The Bible is God's inspired word, they say; take it as if he dictated it verbatim to the Gospel writers. Many still believe that straight-forward simple command. But others, equally believing if somewhat more inquisitive, cannot adhere to the verbal-plenary Doctrine of Inspiration, which I was taught in Seminary many years ago.

The second view, widespread in our time, began in earnest with the Historical Criticism movement in Germany in the late 19th and early 20th Century. This approach is just as committed to the Scriptures, just as avid in seeking to know the word of God, but you have to sift through the details of the four Gospel records— Matthew, Mark, Luke and John— to figure out how they all fit together. There is obviously some overlap and also some apparent contradictions. If our chief glory is to think, then we are called to exercise that glory.

For this chapter, we are located mainly in Luke, although John is still my favorite of the four. It would be easier if Luke were the only author from the 1st Century AD who wrote about the life, death and resurrection of Jesus of Nazareth. We could all smile and say, "Thank you, Luke", and the same to Matthew, Mark and John. But we have all four, and their stories are not unanimous in what took place.

It was not a problem for Billy Graham. I wish I could say the same. Whenever he is preaching the Bible, Dr. Graham concentrates on that portion of God's Word and preaches it as such. Any part of Scripture becomes the be-all and end-all of God's inspired word. Dr. Graham tells in his biography how he never had the time nor the inclination to wrestle with what appear to be conflicts or contradictions in the Scriptures. It is difficult enough to interpret the story, which falls heavily on modern ears, he says, without also having to describe and defend it. Graham is a North Carolina Baptist. He teaches that doubting, even scrutinizing the Scriptures too carefully, is a sin. "When I say 'The Bible says', I get results." "If I were to say, 'I think the Bible says,' or, 'some say the Bible says,' it would just confuse everybody. When I began to preach the Bible and not try to defend it, my success as an evangelist for Christ took root and brought me to where I am," he explained. Others share Billy's point of view.

Neo-orthodox theologian Karl Barth said something similar, even if it was from a different perspective. Barth taught

118

that when discrepancies or contradictions arise, you should read the Bible to find God's word. God will take you by the hand and help you walk the tightrope of life one step at a time. The Lord of All has chosen to do it that way. His Word for you is in the Holy Bible. He will reveal what you need as you read it, through the words or beyond them. Let the arguments and disagreements take care of themselves; the Word of God can take care of itself, too. God will guide you wisely through His Word, step by step. It does not matter what and how the writers of Scripture heard or said or wrote; it only matters that God has decided he will speak to you as you read the Bible.

I have a slightly different point of view. When I read two verses from the Gospels that seem to be at odds with each other, I do not avoid them, nor do I take one and leave the other. I try to understand why they are both in the Scriptures. Come Easter morning, I want to know what happened in the total corpus of the four Gospels, not just one Gospel written at one time. Professor Joseph Fitzmyer was correct when he wrote in his important commentary, "All four Easter Gospel stories begin with the visit of the women to the tomb, but after that, each Gospel goes its own way." Mark says that Mary Magdalene, Mary the mother of James and Salome went up to the tomb. Luke includes the first two, omits Salome and adds "Joanna and the other women." John has Mary Magdalene going to the tomb alone, joined later by John and Peter. Matthew says, "Mary Magdalene and the other Mary went to see the sepulcher."

Luke and John say that the Resurrected Christ appeared in Jerusalem. Matthew says he went back to Galilee. Mark does not have him appear at all, not in the original ending of his Gospel. Matthew seems just as certain that he ascended Easter night. Luke has him ascending 40 days later. John leaves him at breakfast on the shore of the Sea of Galilee (Tiberius), talking to his friends.

Further, the Resurrection appearances of Jesus seem to differ regarding the type of body in which he returned. None of the four writers declares that it was his previous body, like a person on whom CPR had been successfully performed. At times it seems as if the risen body was untouchable. In John, Jesus said, "Do not touch me, I have not yet ascended to my father." In Luke, two disciples walked down the road to Emmaus 17 miles away with the resurrected Jesus walking right beside them, but they did not recognize him. At times he seems to have returned in a spiritual body: for example, he disappeared through closed doors and he came and went at will. But in the same records, he also sat down and ate breakfast with them by the Sea of Tiberius. Forty days later, according to Luke, his resurrected physical-spiritual body flew up into the sky. Mark and Matthew write that a single angel spoke to the women. John and Luke say that two angels were there.

The famous preacher, Alexander Maclaren, accepted all four Gospels as literal truth. "Where you cannot explain the differences, keep reading. If the women have different names, so what, maybe they used nicknames," he suggested. Another writer tried to reconcile the differences by saying that Mary Magdalene got there first, and the others followed. Another writes that Jesus disguised himself so they could not recognize him, to lessen the shock. Another says that he ascended into heaven, came back, and later left again. All agree that whoever was there at the empty tomb would have been puzzled, uncertain and afraid. So are we.

How do you get out of this sort of puzzlement? The Bible

says they were reassured and their faith took wings when "they remembered his words." We need to do that, too. He had told them earlier that he would die on the cross, but that he would rise again. Death would not conquer him. "I will not leave you comfortless. I will come to you," he said. No more guessing, no more wondering, no longer suspended in the neverland between two worlds. The memory of his words came back to help them. At the time he spoke those words, they did not know what he meant or why he spoke them. But when he rose, it all came back. It all fit together. It all made sense. The memory of his words gave them courage to go on.

To shift our focus for a moment, the same thing will happen with the memory of your loved ones and mine; what they said to us while still alive, what they wrote in their letters, the words of encouragement they gave us, what they wanted us to become when the shock of death was over. Memories are all you have left; the things that death can never take away. We can pattern our lives on the best and most encouraging things that have been left for us to hold onto and remember what they stood for. These can carry us on to a new tomorrow.

If all of this takes you to the edge of what you cannot know for sure, remember that the disciples first refused to believe what the women told them. One thing is essential to notice here; the messengers were women in an ancient, male dominated society. Men made all the decisions back then. Women had to live with it. In those days men were supposed to know everything. It was their world. And then came an emotional little group of women telling them that Jesus had come back from the dead.

It bothered early male scholars. In fact, it bothered them so much that some of the later non-canonical gospels, especially those written by the Gnostics, completely eliminated the women from the story. The church became masculine in leadership: male Pope, male pastors, male leaders, male elders and the like. In those later Gospel fragments outside the official canon of the New Testament, the resurrected Christ appears only to men.

They might have said that excitable women are given to flights of fancy or mistakes. "Oh, they probably went to the wrong sepulcher." Luke writes that their words seemed to be "an idle tale." Just like a man to know it all. Men think that women are gullible, that women question less and pray more. The men were not prepared to receive the news that Jesus Christ had risen from the dead. Not only Thomas doubted at the start; they all did.

But the real question here is not what those ancient Disciples thought about the women's idle tale. The real question is what do you believe about the Easter message? Did Christ rise or not? Did God choose this salient moment to be the pivotal turning point of all history, or not? There is not a set of options: it is either yes or no. "You are for me or against me," said the Lord. There is no middle ground, no corner to hide in and no intellectual position to fall back on.

Life is overflowing with miracles. The miracles of life and birth and love and peace are miracles. When you ponder the miracle of life everlasting, it is no greater a miracle than the miracle of the new born baby.

This is not an essay examination. It takes no rocket scientist to figure it out. It isn't even a multiple choice: this, that, or all of the above. This is the easiest test of all, if you know your stuff: true or false. Yea or nay. He rose, or he didn't.

Abraham Lincoln once called his cabinet officers together

for a crucial vote. Then he called for the question and asked for a vote: "All in favor say 'Aye.'" Every member present raised his hand and said, "Aye." Then Lincoln said, "All opposed say 'nay.'" The President himself said "nay." He concluded the meeting by saying "The nays have it." The one vote that matters to eternity is the vote of the Lord. God said "aye" on Easter morning. The one vote that matters to your future is your vote. It is time to cast it!

I know you wanted to be in the chapel this Easter morning. Or maybe you came to please your wife, or your father or who knows who? Maybe you are working today, as I am, by ushering, singing or playing. Or maybe are you trying to please a memory, to find what you used to have or maybe never had, but have heard rumors that it is there. Maybe it is a memory of the lilies in bloom, or the hymn "Jesus Christ Is Risen Today." Maybe you like the sound of the trumpets, or maybe you came to put yourself in touch with something that matters, to test whether what you think you know or do not know is true or false.

The Bible says we cannot live by bread alone. The tangible, touchable things of the here and now are not enough to get us through. The world around us is impatient and unkind. It will let you down. The passing years will get you too. You need a larger view. Sigmund Freud bragged that he could live with just this world alone, no matter what went on, or what came next or didn't. But most people cannot make it on their own. They need to know more or, at least, to explore the option. They want to believe. Try not to be too timid to stand up and accept it.

You ask what the Easter Message can do for you. Can it help me with my marriage? Help me get a job? Help me keep my spirits up? Help me find a boyfriend? Help me with my children? Help me with my depression? What could Easter possibly have to say that could lift me up above it all to a place where everything is fine? I will listen just in case there is something for me to grab hold of, something to put my doubts to rest, something that will let me live in peace."

What happened that first Easter? Not one of the four Gospel writers dared to tell us. Why? Because they did not know. Matthew comes closest. He said there was an earthquake, and the angel rolled away the stone, and when he did, the soldiers were scared to death. Whatever occurred, it was one stupendous, indescribable happening. Pause for a moment and zero in on the first person Jesus appeared to, Mary Magdalene. Suppose that you were Jesus, and they crucified you, and on the third day, as you predicted, you came back to life again. To whom would you appear?

I know it is an impossible question to answer. He had a thousand choices. But he chose her, a woman from the town of Magdala on the southwest coast of the Galilean Sea. When he had met her couple of years earlier, she had been a wreck. The Bible does not say exactly what her malady was, but Luke tells us that she had been possessed by evil spirits and infirmities. Jesus drove seven demons out of her. Who knows how they ever got in? That implies that she was depressed, lost, afraid, lonely, unsure, frightened, devastated. (Luke 8)

But the power of Christ took all that away. When he came by, she became whole and new again. He was Lord of Life before he was Lord of death. He became the Lord of both. Glory be to God! That is the Resurrection power we need to find. When Christ enters, everything else flies away. "It is too simple," a friend of mine once objected. "Every major problem I have ever had always had a simple solution," I told him. Mary became Jesus' most devoted follower. On Friday, when all the Disciples forsook him and fled, Mary Magdalene stayed at the cross until the bitter end. Perhaps he rewarded her faithfulness. Perhaps he liked her. Not to agree with those who conclude that Jesus was married to her, but it was more that he was proud of her.

But Jesus made her the most important person in the world. He did not appear first to Peter or John or to his mother or his brothers. He did not come to Joseph of Arimathea or to Nicodemus. He did not choose Herod or Pilate. He never dropped down to Rome to set Caesar straight. He lavished the newness of his resurrected body on this lovely little gal with the long dark hair who had known endless problems, who once was lost and fearful and alone, until she met the Lord.

The empty tomb did not impress her or anybody else. It upset them. Someone could have stolen the body. The message of the angels—the men dressed in white— did not impress them, either. Doubt and disbelief are everywhere in the Gospels. People saw visions all the time. It was only when they saw the Risen Lord and felt his presence that they believed.

You can fight and argue and wonder about it all day long. You can take half a century to dissect all four Gospels and know most everything about the details. You might think you understand the inspiration of the Scripture. You can get an A+ on every exam in New Testament studies. But unless and until you drop your guard and go over to the Garden and see for yourself, you will have missed it all, and that would be very sad indeed. If I were you, I would go there in my mind and memory. Leap the barriers of this world. If you doubt and disbelieve, take a leap of faith… a leap out of uncertainty. "If Christ is not raised," St. Paul shouts, "your faith is in vain." It would be such a shame for you to miss the moment and the measure of your days, or to miss your Easter Blessing. Try to remember his words: "I will not leave you comfortless. I will come to you. I will rise on the third day. I will take care of you." Try to remember. And in the memory of his words, you will find everything you need for now and forever more. Amen.

XII

ON A CLEAR DAY, YOU CAN SEE FOREVER

*"And very early on the first day of the week
they went to the tomb when the sun had risen…"*
MARK 16:2

On a clear day (we could all sing it together), you can see forever! And Easter is the clearest day of all—the clearest, the bravest, and the best! I pity those who will miss the Easter view. It is too precious, too magnifying, too satisfying not to allow yourself to tip toe into its glory. I do not want you to tumble into tomorrow without taking a long, lingering look at today. On a clear day, you can see forever. On Easter, you can see all the way into eternity. Eternity is a long, long time.

Our title comes from the Broadway musical by Alan Lerner and Barton Lane about Daisy Gamble, a clairvoyant young woman with extraordinary powers. She could conjure up lost objects all by herself. She could make flowers grow by staring at them. She had different views from the rest of us. In the production she sings: "On a clear day you can see forever and ever and ever and evermore." I invite you to take a stand atop the hill of Calvary and enlarge the vision of your body, mind and soul.

Think about some of the clear days of your life, the times when you knew for sure what it was all about, when you believed that everything would turn out right, when you found your purpose for being. Perhaps it was the day you fell in love, or the day you got married (maybe it wasn't, you might be thinking), or the day you realized what God intended you to do and be. Or maybe it was when you took hold of music or the arts or religion or sports, or when they took hold of you. Maybe it was law, teaching, brokerage, medicine, politics, engineering, or perhaps the day you started your own company. Maybe it was the day you decided to be a full-time mother, or the day your first child was born, or the day you got your great promotion.

Maybe it was when you began to surrender your need to control things, when you let go and let God take care of you. Or the day you joined Alcoholics Anonymous, or quit drinking or smoking on your own, or you noticed your diet began to work when you looked in the mirror. Or it could have been the day you began to recover from your grief or your divorce or your ennui, or when you found some new devotion for your time and energy, or when everything came into focus.

Or maybe it was the day you turned your life over to the Lord, when you came forward at a youth rally and asked Christ to come into your heart, and the name Christian became your name. That's a clear day, for sure, a breathtaking day from which you can see forever. I hope you can recall it and embrace it. I hope you still remember it and still value it as your day.

I have a friend who told me he once made a personal commitment to Jesus, but that as he grew older, he came to believe that it was the insecurity of his adolescence that prompted him to take the altar call. "In time, I outgrew the need for that kind of emotional attachment," he told me. I said, "Sammy, you have not outgrown anything; you just abandoned the plan you had at the start."

To see forever... That's what was happening on that first Easter morning. It was not a spring time holiday morning for the people to enjoy, not at all. It was the first day of another week, ho-hum, the first day back at work after a long Passover weekend, a "blue Monday." Everybody was tired and weary. The Passover celebration had been extravagant and gratifying, but by Monday morning, everyone was heading back to the workaday world. If anything important was going to happen on the day after Passover weekend, hardly anyone would notice it. Just like God to do it that way—so unexpected, so surprising and so memorable!

Mark is the shortest and most direct of the Gospels; he proves it in Chapter 16. Very early that morning, on the third day after Jesus died, three women were on their way to the sepulcher to visit the grave of Jesus. But when they arrived and entered the opened doorway, they found that the body of Jesus was gone. They were afraid someone had stolen it.

Then a young man dressed in white told them that Jesus was not there; he had risen from the dead. Pointing to the empty tomb, he said, "See, there is where he used to be. Why do you seek the living among the dead?" Exquisitely simple, wasn't it? Death used to have him, now it no longer does. Simple, but it scared them to death. The three women fled, trembling. In Mark, they told no one what they had seen. They were too frightened. There is no clear view at the end of the Gospel of Mark.

I need to alert you about Mark. He did not go for frills. He was a no-nonsense, straightforward, simple kind of meat-

and-potatoes man. He does not speculate; he does not elaborate. He tells you what he knows, not what he wishes he knew, nor what you might want to hear. Since his was the first of the four Gospel recollections to be written, he did not worry about what the other Evangelists said they saw.

Mark never mentions the birth of Jesus, nothing about the annunciation to Mary or the angels singing out on an ancient hill. They are not his thing. Mark is not big on angels. He mentions in passing that an angel ministered to the Lord in the wilderness (Mark 1). He mentions the "angels in heaven" (Mark 12:25 and 13: 27 & 32). But the only angel who got a speaking part in Mark was the one who sat on the stone outside the empty tomb and told the women that "Jesus is not here; he has risen, as he said." It is almost as if the angel were saying that Jesus had already gone up to be with the creator God. Jesus never appears again in the original writing of Mark, not to anyone. Angels belong more to Luke or John.

Mark does not like theologizing either; he leaves that for John and Paul. If you want to read of the post-Resurrection appearances of Jesus or about his walk with the disciples to Emmaus, try Luke. For a breakfast by the Galilean sea, try John. For the story of the Ascension, try Acts. Do not count on Mark for such heavenly matters.

And I warn you further, even in the simple little Markan story, there are some puzzles. For one thing, it seems that somebody added some verses to the original Mark. In the King James Version and some other modern ones, the last 11 verses of Mark (16: 9-20) are included. But in most reliable and earliest versions, those concluding verses are not there, not footnoted, not entered in italics.

Professor Bart D. Ehrman, in his informative book,

<u>Misquoting Jesus</u>, calls the reasons for rejecting the final vers-
es "solid and indisputable." The literary style of 16:9-20 is
different, to say nothing of the historical fact that in the two
most ancient manuscripts of Mark, the closing passage is not
included. Ehrman, along with other New Testament scholars, speculates that some unknown scribe thought the ending
was too abrupt, likely because it omitted the post-
Resurrection appearances of Jesus. The original ending is so
condescending to the women that many have wondered if
there were possibly a longer ending for Mark that got separated from the original and was overlooked in the subsequent
centuries of scribal copying.

I have often wondered what Mark would answer if we
could question him about the abrupt ending. I think he would
say that he wrote down what he knew at the time. The body
of Jesus was not there. At the time he wrote, it is possible Mark
thought that the Lord had ascended directly into heaven. "I
didn't know then what happened," he might have said.
"Nobody stole the body, though. I talked with everyone."
Remember, Mark was good friends with Simon Peter who had
been there. "Nobody was hiding the body. If the Romans or
the Jews had it, they would have surely produced it within five
minutes after the story of the Resurrection galloped across the
kingdom. They would have tossed his body down on Central
Square in Jerusalem and said, 'See, there he is…dead as dead
can be!'

"And you can be sure none of the Disciples stole it to prove
their point," he would have continued. "That's nonsense.
Would they ever have suffered such persecutions and death, if
they had perpetrated a hoax on themselves? The body was not
there that morning. That I know. More than that, I can tell

you only what I believe, and I believe he rose to heaven, although I never saw it."

You need not be alarmed by all this. I believe in the Resurrection. Mark would tell you he believes it, too. "If Christ is not raised, we are among all men most to be pitied," Paul said. Easter morning in Mark opens in mystery. It ends with fear.

What Mark clearly says is that Jesus the Christ rose up from the dead. He overcame the darkness of mourning with the great shining moment of his rising, a marvelous and unending view, that God intended us to see from the dawn of Creation. The dark was over. The night was gone. Morning has broken. Day is at hand. Spring is here. The fog is lifted. Death is conquered. You can see forever and ever and evermore.

We especially need that view when it comes to the long list of human heartaches. We need a vantage point to see beyond them. Each of us needs a leisurely walk along the top of Calvary to gain a larger vista. We need to gaze beyond the darkness. The Bible opens with Genesis, "Darkness was upon the face of the waters." Once it all was dark. Then God said, "Let there be light," and light there was. On Good Friday afternoon, darkness covered the land. More darkness came that weekend. But then came the gift of light, which God also called forth when the first dawn broke on Easter. The light of the sun can sometimes be so bright that our eyes, accustomed to the night, can hardly bear to look at it.

Some say that Easter is a fabricated story, made up to get you though the darkness. But what we know runs counter to that idea. "At the moment of my greatest need," a tired old woman in a nursing home said to me, "I find God growing nearer to me." "How?" I asked her. She said, "I don't know. I think my weakness helps me." We can get it wrong. When we are the strongest, we know that we are weak. Without the power of Christ to guide us, we stumble along.

Another time, a little country girl from Iowa, when she first visited the towering canyons near the subway stops in New York City exclaimed, "Why, these people have no view! I'd never like to live anywhere where there is no view."

Then, there was the teenager who returned to my study 10 years later to tell me, "The thing that helped me most was when you told me that the darkness would pass, and everything would be okay again." I said, "That helped you?" He said, "Yep it did."

And the young couple who had spent three of their seven years of marriage in marital discord told me, "We would never have made it, Dr. Cromie, if it had not been for what you told us at our wedding. You said that if trouble ever came, we should rush right back to the mountain top of our wedding day, when we could see clearly what we wanted and needed in life." It didn't seem like all that much to me, but I have learned that you need a place to stand and catch your view. You might want to know that this couple is doing fine after 30 years of marriage.

It is preserving the memory of our finest view. It takes a lot of courage. You have to be brave to remain committed. You have to be aggressive to adopt the Resurrection as your own. It doesn't fit with the other things you know. Robert Browning once wrote that if he saw someone walking and talking, who had been buried three days previously, he would be scared to death! He said he wouldn't believe his own eyes. I guess I understand what he meant; but others claim they have been visited from beyond the boundary of death. And the women and the disciples surely did that first Easter morning. Walking through the cemetery is not the kind of thing we like to do, especially if it is still dark; but they did and they were rewarded by his presence.

It could be that some of you do not believe in Christ's Resurrection. Do you ever wonder why? Do you ever try to adjust your view to include it? It could be that you are afraid, afraid to believe. It would upset the applecart of what you think you know. Something alien to your way of understanding things would creep into the center of your soul. But isn't that a funny thing to say? We mourn the passing of the ones we love, and we also mourn the death of Jesus. There is a hint here that some might not have wanted Jesus to return. If we had been there, and we had betrayed him and we had forsaken him and fled, it just could be that it would be easier not to face him again.

Jesus was their dearest friend. It was brave of them to walk up to the tomb while it was still dark, expecting to find his body there. It was braver still to hope that he just might not be there; but that from the hilltop of Calvary, you can see right on through and out the other side. The bravery required here is absolutely monumental. Your courage will result in the view you need.

Contrast that with the passing of another man of peace. Mohandas Gandhi (Mahatma), the great pacifist and leader in India, was assassinated in 1948 by an opponent who detested Gandhi's peaceful ways. The assassin wanted to win the battle by force. He was certain that passive resistance and consultations with the enemy would never lead to victory.

For three days the nation mourned, alternating between

stunned silence and loud wailing. In due time, it was proper for the people to begin to speak. The national poetess, Mrs. Kamala Naidu, spoke for her people with eloquence: "O ba tu," she pined, "O little father, please come back and lead us. We are orphaned forever without your presence on the earth. O little 'Father Gandhi,' please come back and lead us through the dark nights of the present and all the unknown future...Please come back...Please...We are lost without you." A most touching story about one of God's great men. If only Gandhi could come back, all would yet be well. If only...

Thank God no one who has ever seen the Resurrection of Easter morning and shared the clearest view in all the history of the world will ever need to mutter that mournful plea: "Please come back. O little Jesus, please come back, please come back..." No, never! For Jesus is back. He is risen as he said he would. You need never be an orphan on the earth again. Death is not victorious. Our last enemy is gone.

They went looking for a body to fuss over it in memory of the good and lovely things that had passed forever from the earth – or so they thought. They wanted to do some last thing for Jesus, but already he had done every last thing for them. He was standing there and waiting.

But their spirits were so used to mourning, their heads so used to bowing down, their hearts so used to feeling empty, and their sad countenances so used to be trotted out for such a time as this. Their eyes were so filled with tears that they almost failed to see him...almost, until he spoke to them...and then they were brave enough to stop and listen. "Only that day dawns to which you are awake," Thoreau once wrote. I want you to be awake on Easter morning.

They might have missed it had he not spoken to them. I

hope he speaks to you today and that you will listen for his voice or hear the angel say, "Come and see the place where he was, then go and tell them all." Come and see. Go and tell. Receive. Accept. Share. It is yours and mine to have and to give the happy news that Jesus Christ is risen from the dead. He lives, he reigns...and on this clear day, you can see forever, if you choose to. Wipe your tears, lift up your heads and sing Halleluiah. For now and evermore, Amen.

XIII

THE SONG YOU CAN'T FORGET

"By day the Lord commands his steadfast love;
and at night his song is with me."
PSALM 32:08

Once in a while you hear a song you can't forget. It lingers with you; you hum it on the way home or on the way to work or coming out of church. It becomes part of you. It is often uncontrollable; at times you may not even like the tune, but you hum or sing it over and over again, long after it should have drifted off into the wild blue yonder.

Oliver sacks, the widely read neurologist and author of Awakenings, recently wrote a new book about this phenomenon of a song you can't forget. It is titled Musicophilia: Tales of Music and the Brain (Knopf, 2007). Interesting, indeed. While Dr. Sacks is more concerned with abnormal obsessions, he discusses how a tune lingers on in the mind. The repeated recollection is mysterious. Mostly it seems to be unrelated to our conscious desires and preferences. It comes on involuntarily and stays for as long as it wishes. To some it can even become debilitating; to others it is like a little "brainworm" which holds on. St. Augustine also refers to music of the mind and to the music of the spheres, which remembers the song and anticipates the next words, both at once.

It could be a tune that calls up a special memory. My favorite song is <u>Beautiful Dreamer</u>, a Stephen Collins Foster classic, which my mother used to sing to me when I was a little boy. Or it could be a special song that elicits smiles for everything a song can mean. For Peggy and me, that song is "<u>Moon River</u>." I had better never miss it if it is played when we are together.

What music would you choose to hear if this were your last day on earth? A country-western ballad about the <u>Keeper of the Stars</u>? Or something by Willie Nelson, pining for the girls he used to know. It could be a song you used to sing when you were a child, or as a teen, or in a majestic concert hall. Maybe a Sousa March reminds you of Homecoming, Elgar's <u>Pomp and Circumstance</u> and the day you marched down the graduation aisle, Mozart <u>Requiem</u>, Dubois's "<u>Seven Last Words</u>, or any other song that you can't forget. One woman I know hums the theme song from the television show <u>Jeopardy</u> on into the night.

They often sang songs in the Bible. Creation itself is like a symphony. Jubal, the Biblical founder of music, appears early in Genesis. (Genesis 4:21) Moses wrote songs and sang with the people of Israel when they were released from Egypt in the wilderness: "Lord God Almighty, we are free at last." "The Lord is my Strength and my Song" the Psalmist sang. Jesus sang hymns and songs with his disciples. Paul and Silas sang them to the Philippian prisoners to ease their fears. David wrote songs for the people to sing and as a child, sang them to the accompaniment of his harp. "Sing to him a new song", the Psalmist chants. In the last book of the Bible, they are still singing. Combine them all into a song of peace, of hope, of harmony and love, a song that works its way into your soul to remind you of what you were and still can be. Music has a magic all its own. The angels, too, know how to sing. After all, the angelic choir sang on the first Christmas eve.

The song you can't forget. You came on Easter because a song was there, deep within your soul. You came because you had to hear it once again. You used to know the notes and words, but then you moved along. You knew it well before you became so involved in other things, before life took over, before you got confused and became lost in the land of money and success. But that song lingers anyway. It remembers, even when you forget. It acknowledges you as one of its favorite singers. This Easter, I want you to sing that song again: *Jesus Christ is Risen Today!* That should be the song you can't forget.

Today, we could ask the choir to belt out the theme song from Oklahoma, *"Oh, What a Beautiful Morning."* It was a beautiful morning back then at the Garden tomb, and it is a beautiful echo for us. No one on earth knows exactly what happened there. It is lost in the misty morning of long ago when something startling went on before dawn. We search and search the Scriptures, the only reliable source of evidence we have, and still hesitate to declare that we know all the details.

Matthew is explicit about how many doubted. He tells how some of the guards muttered that the stone had been rolled away while they slept, and that some of the elders offered them a bribe to tell the people that Jesus' disciples came by night and stole him away. "So they took the money and they did as they were directed," Matthew wrote, adding, "And this story has been spread among the people to this day" (Matthew 28:15). If you try to master all the details, you will get so weighed down by the complexity of your own disharmony that you will miss the beat of the music. It is a matter of how you came to believe this – or anything else you think you know. The response is more like a song than an academic lecture.

As I read through the Gospel narratives, I am completely convinced that the story is true, but when I pause to wonder why, I find myself asking unanswerable questions. I ask myself how I could be so certain that the Resurrection actually occurred. Some of you will identify with my quest. Others will scoff at it and say it is a matter of faith, not evidence. "Just believe it, Rev!" Others will wonder why a pastor would ask such a ridiculous question. "Of course it's true. It says so in the Bible." It does, but it is not as simple as it appears.

Unfortunately, the "evidence" from the Gospels is not complete, or at least not as consistent as some believers assume. A couple years ago, one of our children asked me, "How do you know it's true, Dad?"

Have you ever wondered how you know anything for sure? Like, how do you know Brutus was there when Julius Caesar was murdered? I first heard it at a high school play. Cicero mentions Caesar frequently, but Cicero is not the most reliable historian. So, how do you know it's true? . . . They say Brutus was persuaded by Cassius to give up his post and participate in the assassination. Shakespeare believed that. They say Brutus committed suicide some years after. But how can you know except that someone wrote it down, and someone you trusted told you about it? In the mystery of what you do and do not believe, using all the integrity and intellectual powers you can muster, you believed it. Not that it matters all that much whether "Et tu Brute," is made up or real, but the whole idea of how you evaluate information and how you come to believe who said what, when, and why continues to intrigue many of us.

Let's shift to the Aegean. I wonder how much I really know

about Socrates and the brilliant things he did and said and believed. He never wrote a word that has survived; he never penned an autobiography that anyone knows of. Some say he was a sculptor; probably he was not. We have heard that he was condemned to death on the charges of corrupting youth with new ideas and of neglecting to worship the gods. They tell us he drank the hemlock willingly and died, seeking to know what was on the other side and guessing that it was favorable. They say he even said that he could die believing that all would be well on the other side. It was better to believe it that way, even if he was wrong. But how do I <u>know</u> that?

Plato and Xenophon wrote about Socrates, but neither of them knew him for more than the last 10 or 12 years of his life. Xenophon admits he was not close to Socrates. Almost everyone agrees that Plato, a loyal disciple, intentionally made his master appear gracious, a part time hagiographer. And Plato often espoused his own ideas through the words he chose for Socrates in the Dialogues, so who really knows what was true?

Or how do I know that the Scotsman William Wallace came down from Aberdeenshire to lead a Scots rebellion that culminated in the victory of Robert the Bruce at Bannockburn in 1413? Of course you can verify it in the popular movie, "Braveheart," but historical novels and motion pictures can hardly be accepted as truth. Not that it would change my life or salvation if the facts were not as I have been told, but my Scottish blood runs more confidently through my veins since I believe it. I know it by what I have been told, by what I have evaluated and received and what I chosen to accept as true.

Pause to think about it in the life and death of Abraham Lincoln. I read once that more has been written about our 16th President than anybody else, save Jesus. Focus on one tiny item.

In Doris Kearns Goodwin's book, <u>Team of Rivals</u>, she writes of the assassination at Ford's Theatre and the President's death in a little boarding house across the street where he had been taken for privacy. As he drew his last breath and died Edward Staunton, Lincoln's stalwart Secretary of War, spoke these final words, "Now he belongs to the ages." It is a widely quoted final word, a lovely tribute, and it came true.

But in the May 28, 2007 <u>New Yorker Magazine</u>, historian Adam Gopnik re-examines the evidence, and finds alarming discrepancies in what people said happened that evening. In James L. Swanson's intensive book about the death of Lincoln, Stanton is quoted as having said: "Now he belongs to the angels." Such discrepancies need not detain us now; they simply add to the question we are discussing here. Even with the death of a most public president whose appointed scribe was present, no one can be exactly sure what his final words were.

So, how do I <u>know</u> anything, and how do you? How do you even know that your wife or husband or children love you? Perhaps they send you flowers or gifts or birthday cards. Perhaps they say nice things to you (and of course they are true). Some families end conversations automatically with "I love you" – "I love you, too." But sometimes along the way, it does not turn out that way. What was declared as a love it turns out was not a real love after all.

We are diverging from my original thoughts. What I am trying to say is that almost everywhere you turn when we look at the history of philosophical and scientific ideas, what appears to be true at one time can be declared false at another. Facts that we accept at one time are later shown to be wrong. As I write this, I think of poor little planet Pluto, recently declared NOT to be a planet after all.

My point in this introduction is that in order to believe any-thing, we have to depend on written and oral evidence and on the private receptor system inside us, perhaps genetically preconditioned, which helps us to select what we come to believe. It takes a leap of faith in a thousand other areas of human activity, not only in theology, to believe what is true and what is not.

This brings me to the subject of Easter and the Resurrection of Jesus Christ. Many of us here accept it as fact without dispute. That's fine. My mother was like that. She often told me not to bother her with new ideas. "I know what I believe, and I don't need my son to mix me up!" she would say. Others think of Easter mainly as an inspirational story, made up by the Disciples to get them through their grief and embarrassment. Those in between drift to and fro. Some affirm a physical resurrection; some a spiritual one; still others stop at the psychological change in the Disciples brought on by their belief that Jesus had risen from the dead.

With all that in mind, let me set forth a case for what I believe happened on the first Easter.

First, Jesus of Nazareth died. If you read the records of the Resurrection in the New Testament, four in the Gospels and two beyond, there can be no doubt that following the crucifixion Jesus was dead. Some early Christian scholars later speculated that it only appeared that he had died. The Gnostics could not accept that the Son of God could actually die. Yet the Gospel writers all tell how he breathed his last. The soldiers who came to break his legs to help death along saw that he was already dead, so "not a bone in his body was broken". When Joseph of Arimathea and Nicodemus took the body down, Pilate ordered a centurion to verify that Jesus was dead (Mark 15:43). He did. He was. From all evidence we have, Jesus was dead.

Second, <u>the tomb was empty when they arrived</u>. If you read the four Gospels, there can be no doubt that the body of Jesus Christ was gone. The tomb had been sealed, and soldiers were there to guard the place. The authorities were fearful that the Disciples might steal the body. Matthew is the only canonical writer who attempts to tell us how the Resurrection happened. A great earthquake came, he wrote, and an angel came down, rolled away the stone and sat on it. The guards were so shocked, they pretended to be dead. No one saw it happen. The 2nd century theologian Ignatius wrestled with this and concluded that, "Our Lord rose in the silence of God." The other three Gospel writers would agree.

Some women came to the tomb on Easter morning. The Gospels differ on who they were. That is puzzling, but at least it proves that there was no conspiracy to present a unified story. Peter and John agree that the body was gone. John himself (or more accurately the author of John) writes that when he entered the sepulcher, the body of Jesus was gone. Where was it? Neither his friends nor his foes had taken it.

The third piece of evidence arises out of <u>what happened next to the Disciples</u>, as the Christian church began to grow. If they had fabricated the story, they would hardly have been devoted enough to surrender their lives for a lie. They had nothing to gain in sharing their stories, other than their conviction that it was true. In those early decades, his Disciples lost everything. Dramatically, each was given a chance to change the story. All they would have had to do was make a statement of faith in the Emperor's gods, even a token affirmation would do, and they would have escaped execution. They refused.

Luke was a literary scholar. He was not an eyewitness. When he heard stories of Jesus, he went and interviewed those who were eyewitnesses. He examined the evidence. We owe him a great debt. He became a companion to St. Paul, following him everywhere and risking his own life. Why? Because of the Resurrection. I Corinthians 15 says, "If Christ is not raised, your faith is futile."

What persuaded Luke in the end is exactly what could persuade the rest of us. Jesus was a kindly healer. He cared about those in trouble. He taught people how to live a life which is grounded in love. But that was not enough for Luke, as it is not enough for me and you. The German philosopher Ernst Bloch, a critic of the faith, wrote, "Christianity was not in competition for a set of good morals. His followers were not passing on the message that we should try to do better. The competition was for eternal life and how we can receive it and possess it."

There were critics at the beginning. The Jews in Jerusalem thought it blasphemous that anyone sensible would conclude that a crucified criminal could be the Messiah. To the cultured educated Greeks, the "soul" alone could be immortal, once it shed its weak and repugnant body. The Gnostics taught that Jesus was an immortal spirit, masquerading around in a pretend body.

And there are critics around us now, as there have always been. One leading Christian New Testament scholar, the German Gerd Ludeman, teaches that the resurrected body was a subjective vision produced by Simon Peter's psyche to overcome his grief and guilt. Others teach that the Risen Christ culminates a series of inter-psychic experiences. An often misguided professor actually teaches that the body of Jesus was stolen by wild beasts, and that only a vision remained.

Fourth and last, <u>there were thousands then, and have been millions ever since, who accept the</u> <u>conclusion that Jesus Christ is Risen from the dead</u>. After examining the evidence and examining their hearts, they <u>know</u> it is true. I am part of that innumerable company who, once having examined the evidence, came down on the side of belief. I will match my wits and arguments and "evidence" with anyone, anywhere, at any time.

As we close, let's return to my original question: How do you know the things you think you know? How do you come to believe the things you believe? Well, you talk with eyewitnesses if you want to know what happened. Not that each would tell the identical story, but usually the stories overlap.

After that, you need to evaluate what you read and "know." Finally you have to work it through your own body, mind and soul. Then, you have to make a choice. The Biblical accounts of Jesus' life, death and resurrection were written by those who were there. They tell us what they saw and knew and believed.

The rest is up to you. Take it or leave it. Take it, and nothing else will matter more in all your life. Leave it, and you leave everything you need behind. Argue about the details all day long. Test your faith. Be prepared to give an account of the faith that is within you. But for goodness sake, join the victorious company who came to believe what happened on the first Easter morning. If you have a choice between life and death, choose life.

And go away singing the song you can't forget. No matter that the earth itself should be removed, no matter that the mountains be carried into the midst of the sea, no matter that the waters roar and be troubled, no matter what else goes wrong, whatever else has happened, is happening, or will happen, Christ is risen! He is risen indeed! The "Hallelujah" is a chorus. Let's sing it – now and forevermore.

Amen.

XIV

THOMAS IS A FRIEND OF MINE

"Blessed are they that have not seen, and yet they have believed."
JOHN 20:29

Thomas is a friend of mine. I like him. I think you would have liked him, too. He was a twin; they called him Didymus, which means twin in Greek. I wish we knew something of his twin brother. Twins are special people. My father was a twin.

Thomas was inquisitive. We learn from John 14 that when Jesus said the comforting words, "Let not your hearts be troubled; you believe in God, believe also in me. In my father's house are many rooms; if it were not so, I would have told you that I go to prepare a place for you....And you know the way where I am going." Thomas interrupted him and said, "Lord we do not know where you are going; how can we know the way?" This prompted Jesus to teach them, "I am the way, and the truth, and the life. No one comes to the father, but by me." Those are confident, lovely and enduring words.

Thomas was also brave beyond expectations. When Jesus decided to go up to Bethany to heal Lazarus (dangerous as it was, for the authorities were looking to arrest him), it was Thomas who said to his fellow disciples, "Let us also go, that we may die with him" (John 11:14-16). Thomas was loyal. Where I grew up, loyalty was the first and finest virtue of a friend.

The Bible does not say where Thomas was at the time of the crucifixion. I guess we can assume that like the other disciples (with the exception of The Beloved Disciple at the foot of the cross), Thomas was with those who forsook the master and fled. It also does not say where he was when the Risen Jesus came back to reveal himself to the Disciples on Easter evening (John 20:24). It could be that he needed to grieve alone; before he could comfort others, he had to find comfort himself. I know people like that.

When they told him that Jesus had visited them, he did not believe them. (Wait a minute Thomas. These are your fellow Disciples who followed the Lord alongside you.) The Gospel tells us that Thomas said, "Unless I see in his hands the print of the nails, and place my finger in the mark of the nails, and place my hand in his side, I will not believe" (John 20:25).

Thomas was someone who was quick to question what other people say. I know many others like him. He was made and trained to make decisions on his own. He took hold of almost nothing he had been told, unless he could verify it on his own. He had to see before he could believe.

I wonder what you think of that, or what you think of those you know who are just like him. Let me remind you, before we go further, that old Thomas is my kith and kin, a fellow traveler on a road I often trod. He is a friend of mine, and I will defend him to my dying day and, should God let me, even after that.

Throughout the centuries, Thomas has been maligned as the one who had doubts about the Resurrection of our Lord.

"Doubting Thomas" is the epithet we use to stifle any honest reservation, to shush any probing question; it is the barb we use to nail down the edges of our guilt, as if it were somehow more Christian to accept everything on sight and never ask a question, no matter what you think or feel, for fear that someone more believing will make fun of you.

Meanwhile, I like an honest man or woman. I think there is a secret touch of Thomas deep within most of us. Every time we use the brain God gave us to stretch a little further, every time we peek over the edge of disbelief, every time we cannot understand and want to know some more, the patron saint we need to hold our hand is Didymus, the twin.

Thomas was rigorous in his search for truth, but in the end he found it, or even better, his faith found him. Like Mrs. Darwin said after Charles had written <u>The Origin of the Species</u>, "I don't know if he believes in God and all the miracles, but I still think that Christ believes in him."

* * * * *

Thomas was a cautious man who finally found his place in following Jesus. But just when he had it, it was gone! A sudden death has a way of doing that. It does not fit our categories of what is good and right and fair. It cannot, does not, fit into the framework of it all. Paul calls death the last enemy, and a sudden death brings even greater uncertainty and shock.

Thomas was the kind of man who liked to solve problems by himself. He was not present when Christ came the first time. But a week later, he was with the Disciples in the same upper room when Jesus suddenly appeared among them. How Jesus got there, no one knew; apparently he could drift through doors without opening them. Anyway, he looked at Thomas and said, "All right, Thomas, put your finger here. What happened to your faith?"

Thomas shuddered and answered, "I have been a fool. My Lord and my God, you're really here!" Cautious he was, but he was not dumb. He did not make a fetish of his doubt. He was a seeker, but when he found the one he sought, his seeking days were done. He would not pretend, but after he saw it, he believed.

We had better clarify another point before we go much further: I am not trying to convince you or to coerce you into believing the events of Resurrection morning. To argue for the empty tomb would be a foolhardy exercise, and I am sure the empty tomb can argue for itself. It needs no defense from me. The empty tomb is not the final proof of whether Christ is risen anyway. The final stroke, which ties the knot for good, is the personal testimony of those who actually saw and now believe. In the Scripture, the empty tomb provokes nothing but dismay. It provides nothing consequential. It proves only that the body was not there.

• • • • •

I hesitate to say it, but a careful reading of the Easter story in the Gospels creates some difficulties. It all begins in darkness. When he returned to them on Easter evening, Jesus startled them by his sudden appearance; they thought they were seeing a ghost. Later, he walked with a couple of his followers out to Bethany where he blessed them and "He parted from them, and he was carried up into heaven" (Luke 24:50). Naturally, the Disciples returned to Jerusalem with great joy.

John says that Mary stood weeping outside the tomb, when two angels dressed in white sitting on the funeral catafalque (one at the head and one at the feet) asked her why she was weeping. She said," Because they have taken away my Lord and I do not know where they have laid him." Then she turned around and saw Jesus standing there, but she did not know that it was Jesus (John 20:14). Jesus said to her, "Woman, why are you weeping? Whom do you seek?" Supposing him to be the gardener, she said respectfully, "Sir, if you have carried him away, tell me where you have taken him, and I will take him away." (She wanted to give him a proper permanent burial.)

Then Jesus said to her, "Mary." When he spoke her name, she recognized him and tried to touch him. He said, "No, do not hold me." Then, curiously, he added, "I have not yet ascended to the father."

Later in John, he appeared to the Disciples, and he came back to visit Thomas. (John writes that he did many other things in the presence of the Disciples that are not written in his book. Oh, would that they were.) Finally, one morning on the shore of the Sea of Galilee (which John calls Tiberius), he cooked a farewell breakfast for some of the Disciples who had gone up to Galilee. Thomas was among them. There The Lord gave Simon Peter three commands to share his love.

Of course, by including these varying details I do not mean to cast suspicion on the story. In fact, the slight differences in the stories only verify their truthfulness. If it had been a fabricated story, it would have lost its excitement and its spontaneity. It was hardly contrived. There was no conspiracy to make all the loose ends fit. There were four separate traditions recollecting this amazing event, like four fine paintings of the same lake. It does cause some problems, even for a believer, but none are insurmountable. All four renditions are of the same occurrence.

Matthew refers to the rumor that the disciples had stolen

the body, and some who saw it, Matthew says, still did not believe it. They were not naïve. Doubt is not new. Samuel Butler's hero in <u>The Way of All Flesh</u>, the clergyman's son, lost his faith when confronted with this varied evidence and became an agnostic.

In my case, it makes my faith greater. The eminent New Testament scholar Rudolph Bultmann shocked the world by writing of the "incredibility of this mythical event of the resuscitation of a corpse." But Bultmann admits that something happened that changed the Disciples' attitude— the "X" factor, as Dibelius once called it. "X", my foot! What recreated their joy after the dismal events of Friday afternoon? The "X" factor, Christians have always believed, was Christ's Resurrection, his return from the dead. It is not so much the empty tomb as it was the witness of those who actually *saw* the Lord that counts. It was not wrong for Thomas to want to see.

The earliest mention of the Resurrection, by the way, is not in any of the Gospels. It is in Paul's letter to the Corinthians written around 55 A.D. No one knows when the Gospels were written, but it is certain that it was 30 years or so after the resurrection before the first one appeared. John is assumed to be the last one written, and it could have come as late as 90 or 100 A.D.

When St. Paul lists the testimony of those who actually saw the Lord, he writes, "He appeared to Cephas, then to the twelve (eleven really), then to five hundred most of whom are still alive (in case you want to check with them) though some have fallen asleep, then to James, then to all of the apostles". . . . then (watch it!) "last of all, as to one untimely born, he appeared to me." Paul never said he "saw" the Lord. He meant that his vision of Christ on the road to Damascus was an appearance of equal value with that of the Disciples and the

500 others. When he chose the words "was raised" from the dead, he was saying Jesus was raised by an intervention in an act of God. Jesus Christ was changed from one mode of existence to another, from what Paul calls the perishable to the imperishable, from the mortal to the immortal. Everyone from Peter onward through Paul saw something of the same.

When Paul writes that Jesus was raised and that he appeared, what he means is not that his mortal body was miraculously resuscitated, but that his whole self, his persona, his presence, was transformed. It was not gone. It was changed, but Jesus was still recognizable. And from his new eschatological dwelling place (or rather in it) he was truly there — and here — not in the body as we know it, but in a transcendent body. It was not an abnormal vision either, not a hallucination or projection from the sky: the Risen Christ was really there in a way that produced personal encounters. They saw him. He was there.

Deep down inside all of us, there is a longing to believe that our lives, our personalities, will not end when death intrudes. We long to attach ourselves to something beyond the limits of this ordinary life, however long it lasts on earth. At our core, we all need something to believe in; we need an Easter morning, not just a springtime of our spirits, which comes and goes each year as the pretty flowers grow and the birds nest again and the warm sun and spring rains turn the fields into blossom. Spring is a blessing, to be sure, but Easter is more than spring! We need to know that all is well eternally, giving us some inner assurance and security about what our lives mean, where it all is going and how we too might get there.

Then along comes Easter morning, "the land where the great mists lie and the great rivers spring," said old Principal

Cairns of the University of Aberdeen.

Now it all would be unbelievably incredible, my friends, if it stood alone, like an isolated one time event that defied all the other human things we know. The mythical stories of gods and men who came back to life are legendary. Toynbee tells of 168 parallels with the life and death and resurrection of Jesus in other ancient religions. When I first read Mueller's The Uses of the Past, my faith went spinning like a top. He tells of the cult of Mithra. Too many items in the life of Mithra reflect what we believe happened in the life and death of Jesus.

I do not cite these sources to alarm you, but to let you know that Thomas has been my friend for more years than you could ever guess. Christ's affirmation of Thomas in the middle of his doubt has always been a special gift to me. I often wander out to the abyss of doubt. As I mentioned Nietzsche once warned that if you stare too long into the abyss, it will begin to stare back. It does. But I usually come back smiling.

If the resurrection of Jesus were the only miraculous event we ever heard about, that would make a difference. But it isn't. From one angle, it is not even the greatest miracle in the Bible. It follows a long line of mighty and miraculous things which began way back in Genesis. There, it tells of the creation of the universe. That must be the greatest miracle of all: out of nothing the whole world came to be. God created the heavens and the earth and the crown of all creation, human life ex nihilo.

That first stir, that God-generating movement, set the stars on their courses. Then people came along, with their societies and their self-governance. Then (as Teilhard noticed) the birth of love, concern, and peace all came to be from that; they were imbedded in the beginning. Some scoffer would say it would be impossible. Each time a newborn child arrives, from the act of procreation, in only a few months it forms itself and then comes to greet the world, carrying within it seeds enough to form an adult and bring on the following generations, the movement of its brain, its heart, its hopes, all of them and more. Is that not a miracle?

When Harlow Shapely, the great astronomer at University Park, Pennsylvania, looked at all the possibilities of what might have happened in the formation of the universe, he concluded that it was impossible that human beings could ever arise out of the dust of the earth. "Human life coming to the earth by accident is equivalent to a Webster's unabridged dictionary resulting from a mad explosion in a printing shop," he said. And I laugh when I recall the 10-year-old in his modern class on all things sexual. When told how babies really come, he said, "That sure is funny; I'd rather believe in the stork!"

That should speak to the little Thomas doubting within you. Whether the Resurrection could or could not have occurred is not the issue. If the Creator God could make a universe, surely he would have the skill and power to bring a man back to life after his breathing had stopped. I think we know *something* happened, we just wonder who or what it was.

What started life and why? Who set it all in motion? Random happenings? Of course not! That is nonsense! Who sets the stars upon their courses? Who taught the birds to fly? Who knows the mighty deeps that form the ocean's restless waves? Is it any more incredible to think of life itself than to think of life eternal? Is it any more a miracle that a life comes back (or goes on) after death, than that life begins in the first place?

Harry Williams at Cambridge explained that one aspect of our problem is that we try to isolate the Resurrection. We fix it in a moment's time 2000 years ago, or ponder over what will come in some future resurrection for me. It is but one of many moments consistent with the resurrection movement in which we see in the birth of all creation, and in the birth of every individual life and in each new moment of each day. Every time new hope is born, it is a kind of mini-resurrection. Every time a child comes home from wandering far away from self, it is a mini-resurrection. Every time a broken dream is mended or a broken relationship restored, or illness overcome, every time a tired old marriage takes on new life again, every time we rise up after we have fallen on our faces there is an inkling of the first Resurrection morning.

Easter is not all that incredible or unusual. It belongs to the sanctity of life, part of God's unfolding story of the power and purpose here on the earth. If not, it is all a hoax; and while I could live with that if it were forced on me and trudge on anyway, it is surely better to step out in trust, believing where we cannot see. Hurrah for Thomas when he finally opened up his eyes!

I take the Resurrection of Jesus as a gift. We do not deserve it, we never earned it and we cannot earn it now. I am not an essentially trusting person. I am often too critical and analytical. I make decisions carefully. But Karl Barth once taught me that all revelation comes from the Scripture as a gift. One weighs the evidence, seeks God's guidance, but then one must decide. It is too great a decision to let it hang in limbo. It is too important a journey for you and me to stand bewildered at the crossroads waiting, watching, hoping for now and evermore.

I also believe in the Resurrection because it is not an isolated event. It belongs to a far larger question than that of whether Jesus arose from the dead. It has to do with the total story of what God has in mind. Everything I believe about the miracle of creation and about the miracle of life, about what God is doing in his world fits together.

Those who were around when Jesus returned said, "We saw the Lord." They were privileged. It would have been wonderful if you and I had been there, too. That would have settled it. Or maybe, like Thomas, we would have had our doubts even then. I wonder if that speculation is true, because many who saw it still did not believe. They did not think it was possible for dead men to get up again. If the other miracles of God do not inspire or impress you, this one will not either.

The path which Thomas took began with an honest search for truth, but it leads to somewhere else beyond. It asks for a decision. Thomas was quite cautious, but Thomas was not dumb. When he heard and weighed it all, when he finally found the eyes to see it, he put down his guard and waltzed along with power and with peace to a marvelous affirmation. Without touching Jesus, he declared, "My Lord and my God."

That is why Thomas is a friend of mine. "Because Thomas doubted", Augustine said, "I do not have to doubt anymore." Jesus said, "Have you believed because you have seen, Thomas? Blessed are those who have not seen and yet believe." And blessed, I remind you, means happy! For now and for evermore. Amen.

XV

SOMETIME BEFORE THE DAWN

"Now on the first day of the week, Mary Magdalene came
to the tomb early, while it was still dark, and saw that
the stone had been taken away from the tomb."
JOHN 20:1

How sad and distraught and lonely Mary Magdalene must have felt as she eased out of her little home sometime before the dawn that first Easter morning to venture to the garden grave-yard at the foot of the Mount of Olives. She was going for her first visit to the sepulcher where Joseph of Arimathea had placed the body of Jesus just two days before. On that day, the worst agony she had ever experienced had come thundering into her fragile little world, and that God-forsaken emptiness lingered and dogged her every step all weekend long. "It just cannot be…"

Forty-eight hours is not even enough time for the initial shock to wear thin. Sometimes the first two days slip out of memory for good, so staggering and so overwhelming they are when you lose someone you love. He is a risen Lord to us, we know how the story ends – or at least I hope you do. But to her, he was the dearest one in the world. And he was gone.

Maybe she was going there to weep, or to feel a little closer to him. Why do people visit graves anyway? I come from a cemetery-visiting, grave-decorating family. Since childhood, when my Dad took the four of us down to Allegheny Cemetery where his mother was buried, I have had a fascination with visiting gravesites. What is certain is that Mary felt like a spectator looking in from the outside, a stranger to her own body, numb within, afraid without. We all respond by rote sometimes, and shock can stem the tears.

I would guess that she had been up all night and the night before; preparing the spices, fidgeting, fussing, wasting away the hours until the dawn, which it seemed would never come. People have told me that nights are bad, but mornings can be worse at the start: a whole new day lies ahead, and it is still true: the grief is still there. Things had thundered in on Good Friday, bad day filled with shouting and hooting and jeering. How could people ever watch so despicable and cruel an event as a crucifixion? Then after Jesus died, a huge stone was rolled in front of his tomb. According to Mark, the other women were worried about how they would be able to remove the stone when they got there. It happened so fast, so shoddily, those sacrilegious Romans and poor Jews hurrying a thing like the preparation of a body just so that the sun would not go down on their misdeed.

It was only fitting and proper that Jesus' body should have had some special treatment; that's the way things were done in ancient Palestine. Sure, the body is only a casing to house the person; but it holds the only person we will ever know. Without that body, we could never live the first life, let alone live on forevermore. The stuff of today is the stuff out of which immortality is made. Bodies are important to Christians.

160

Without hands and hearts and eyes and words, you would not be you, and I would not be me. When St. Paul speaks of the Resurrection, he says a "resurrection of the body," just like we say each week in the Apostles' Creed. Neither Paul nor Jesus denies us the body, the visage that makes us who we are; Jesus traded it for an imperishable one.

Think of Mary, brokenhearted, anxious, even angry, so ready to go and see, she could not wait a minute longer. So while it was still dark, some time before the dawn, she wrapped her homemade shawl around her shoulders and pushed out of her mud house to edge through the cold chill of the early morning to visit the gravesite of her Lord.

It was so tragic, the way it had ended. All their vaunted hopes and glories, all the expectations the disciples and others had that this time would be different now had to be changed. Everything they dreamed of being and becoming was invested in the person and presence of Jesus Christ. The One to set it right was there and made it all worthwhile. Then it all tumbled down that dusty hill of Golgotha. Their ship was listing, the rudder broken and the Captain dead. The one remaining symbol was his silenced body, which had breathed and laughed and loved and healed her, and was now lying in a dark, cold tomb. Mary Magdalene and the disciples were alone. Imagine their pondering: God must have something great in store, but what could it possibly be?

Meanwhile, though, there was this one little chore and customary veneration. "There's something I can do," thought Mary Magdalene. "I will find the other women, and we will go by the grave and place our spices and our flowers there." So on the first day of the week, sometime before the dawn, out she went.

I lived and studied at St. Mary's College in St. Andrews, Scotland, on the North Sea. Sea fog in Scottish is called "the haar." Professor Donald Baillie, who used to teach there, once likened the attempt to discover truth and understand theology to looking through the haar, which comes sweeping in off the North Sea. It diminishes the view. It makes it difficult to see. But if you look closely enough, you will understand that "while you cannot see through the fog clearly, you can see." You just have to concentrate harder. You can see.

The Disciples and the others were in their rooms, which gave them shelter from their fears and safely housed their broken hearts. When Jesus arose, no one else was there to monitor the crowds, and guards of every age are known to sleep at night. No one was there to announce it to the world. No one got the "scoop." There were no eyewitnesses to report what happened. We must surmise the way it happened.

One lovely little non-canonical Gospel fragment says that the stone rolled itself away. I like that. Another speculates that two angels came and moved it. But the act of Resurrection belongs to no one in particular, for it belongs to everyone. That single moment is common property, a common wellspring from which each and every one of us can draw the living water that we need.

You know what happened next, as we reach the crowning capstone of the Scripture: this is what it's all about. In both testaments, all 66 books, 1189 chapters, all 1290 pages, 31,173 verses, all 773,692 words written over 1300 years: this is the key that unlocks it all; this grand event of Easter. This is the code that gives us the right to know what it is all about. It answers the conundrum of why human sin will never go away. It answers the question why the world was made the way God made it. It answers everything you want to know. This is what God has done, is doing, and will continue to do forever more, through the whole pattern of change—growing up and growing old and growing bad and growing good and growing God-like and growing man-and-woman-like.

This is what it is all about: one verse, one stanza, one celestial song, one great refrain, one line, one soul, one faith, one word, one birth, one Jesus Christ, one Easter Morning!

When the women got there, it says, the stone was already rolled away. Some time ago, I was near Collingswood, New Jersey, at Harleigh Cemetery, where I had journeyed to bury the father of a friend. There I came across a tomb in the garden, to the left of the entrance and down a winding road. It is the burial place of Walt Whitman. He celebrated death as well as life, within the self and out of it, and more clearly than any other native poet got the message about the things that death can never touch. Walt Whitman's songs are worth the singing.

But it is not the grandeur of Whitman's songs that we will seek to sing this morning. It is only the image of his tomb I hope to take you to. Picture it with your mind's eye, if you have never seen it down there, just across the road, shielded by an oak tree, and nestled gently back into the hillside behind the cedars and the daffodils. There you will find Walt Whitman's private mausoleum. It is worth the visit. I shall go back that way again myself one day. Whitman is buried there with his parents and some other family members. In addition to blending into a hillside, it has an added feature: the sepulcher itself is guarded against entry and the various and sundry desecrations known to happen in our time. It has a huge iron gate, padlocked to the teeth. I think Whitman would smile at that, as if somehow he would guess that they were trying to keep him in, not keeping others out.

Just to the right of the iron gate, as if it were a giant door swung open, taller than any man and broader than its width, is a huge granite stone which, from my research, I discovered is as close to the kind of stone that covered the grave in which Jesus lay long ago on that Friday night and Saturday, and from which he rose on the morning of the third day.

I saw a symbol there, just a symbol. It is as if that architect of the grave site was saying, "We cannot contain Walt Whitman in a tomb, so in symbol, let's roll that stone back and allow him to be free to go in and out with pleasure." And as Whitman wrote himself — oh, I love these words of the dedication to the one poem you should read if you read no other one of his:

Song of Myself:

Come, said my Soul,
Such verses for my Body let us
    Write, (for we are one,)
That should I after death
    invisibly return,
Or, long, long hence,
    in other spheres,
There to some group of mates
    The chants resuming,
(Tallying Earth's soil, trees,
    winds, tumultuous waves,)
Ever and ever yet the verses
    owning – as, first, I here
        and now,
Signing for Soul and Body, set to
    them my name.
                    WALT WHITMAN

Aye, Walt, you did! And no graveyard there on Harleigh's mound can hold your soaring interest in the precious gift of life.

With that as our backdrop, I go on to say three short things:

First: don't get all bogged down in the why and how and whether of the Resurrection. It will not do you any good. Even if you could find the proof to make it logical, or find some proof that it be not true, you would be left exactly as you are. That's just our trouble. Our scientific day has need to verify the things around us that can confuse their ultimate worth. Our methods and our logic become the guides we use to monitor the miracles and messages that the Lord God has in mind. But the power and the grace of God cannot be contained within our scientific symbols any more than the poetry of Whitman can be contained behind the stone in Harleigh.

It is enough to say that something marvelous and magnificent happened. It is enough to say it, and those who are unprepared to believe it or afraid to lean on something less than positive, logical proof, well, let them live with the version their sagging souls can muster. That's their problem. This is our moment. And in the dark of life, let's swing our arms together as we head out to that lovely little garden and the tomb where the body of our Lord was laid.

I once heard the echo of an ancient Easter legend concerning a band of fallen angels who were asked what they missed most. "Ah," they said, "the sound of the trumpets on Easter morning." To the rest, it is the noise of battle or of pomp and circumstance.

Secondly, try not to fall prey to the critics who say that believing in the afterlife lessens the significance of this life here on earth. What's a heaven for, if it does not give zest and nobility to the years we live on earth? The mind of God retains it all. Sophie Tucker said some great words in paying tribute to Irving Berlin when she wrote: "What a wonderful feeling it must be to know while you're still alive that you are immortal!" Easter says that, too. While we are still alive, we have already entered into eternal life. While we are still alive, we are immortal. That's not tame and ecclesiastical. Just imagine how it can move out to change the world. The world moves aside for men and women who know where they are going. What a great thing it would be if we believed in the eternal importance of each moment. What if we took the good news of the Gospel out to all the world and shared everything we have and are in acts of kindness to those who need us? What if we could say to our political, social, emotional, business, labor problems, "I have seen the Lord. He gives my life its meaning. Now, let's sit down and talk."

Professor Esther Benson once wrote of the Etruscan civilization which affirmed the belief, in the 6th Century B.C., of death and immortality. Their paintings on the walls of the burial tombs were joyous with a celebration of life. Two hundred years later, that civilization had changed its beliefs, and when they did, their lives and their art work became gloomy and clumsy. The afterlife ceased to be a continuance of the journey of life with all its wonder, to be repeated and renewed and raised. Instead, it became terrifying, and afraid of life, they became afraid of death. The Roman spirit of the existential destroyed the soul and heart and beauty of their ancient way of life. It matters to eternity what we do today. This life is not cheapened when we reach out to everlasting life beyond. It is ennobled. It is enhanced. Otherwise, we are like arrows shot by an unknown bowman to fall we know not where. The very thing that gives life meaning is our belief that our lives are precious and enduring and live on forever more.

Thirdly, the message of Easter, in its largest setting, is the triumph of good over evil, then over now, life over death, God over mine, the affirmation of what can be over what we are, magnificence over meanness. The only view that will be sacred ever after is the view that can look beyond and above and around the vicissitudes, vagaries and vagueness of this often weak and sorry life, where almost everything under the sun can happen, and often does, for the worst. We need to claim the dream, to hold it all together. You can kill the dreamer, but you cannot kill the dream. You can execute the messenger, but the message lingers on. You can silence the singer, but the song will echo in your ears on down the coming years.

Ben Franklin wrote his own epitaph. It said, "The body of Benjamin Franklin, Printer (like the cover of an old book, its contents torn out and stripped of its lettering and gilding, lies here. . . but the work shall not be lost, for it will appear once more in a new and more elegant edition, revised and corrected by the Author." From Franklin's Biography.) That's a mini-image of the Easter faith.

In the Anthony Burgess adaptation of the life of Christ on television there is a scene where John the Baptist was in prison. While it does not appear in Scripture, it made a penetrating point. Herod Antipas said to John, "Baptist, what would you be willing to do, if I should set you free?" John replied, "I would go back and follow the one whose way I have recently prepared. Without a single pause, if you would set me free, I should go on to live and serve the Christ, and if I should die today, I would miss all the tomorrows wherein I might serve my Lord."

If Christ should free you, what would you do then, or if he has freed you, what will you do now? That is your question, too, my friend, and mine, even as we live in a different frame of mind, and in a far different time and place. The question should haunt your every footstep for the remainder of this day and all the days to come. "If one who has the power should free you, what would you do?"

Wait a minute: why the "IF? " The conditions have changed as surely as the time and place have. If God should free you from the prison of your fears, what would you do? If God should turn it all around so that you can join with the company of the saints, who have in their own ways seen the Lord healed and whole and risen, what would you do if you could be freed from your fear of life and death? But why the "IF"? Make it SINCE we have been freed, SINCE the heavens and the earth are shouting, "All is well," SINCE the battle's finally won, what will you change about yourself? Will it make any difference to you?

So our story is done, and now you can go on your way. But let's take one last look before we say goodbye to that first Easter. The sun finally rose up that morning. The dawn's early light came to ease the chilly darkness away. Daybreak finally arrived. The angel messengers went back into heaven, I guess. Someone probably rolled the stone back into place again. It was business as usual down in Jerusalem. The morning was awakening the ancient city to be up and at it once again on the first day of that new week. It was time to go back to waiting chores—jobs to attend, fires to warm, wares to hawk in the marketplace, compromises to make.

For most of them, it was very much the same as any other day. It started looking just like all the rest. Tell me, how do you recognize the exceptional days anyway; they begin just like any other day; they arise in ordinary clothing, unannounced, without fanfare, without warning.

I failed to tell you what happened next to Mary Magdalene. You can see her now, since the sun has risen. Already on the move on that little hillside near the lovely slopes at the foothills of the Mount of Olives, the young woman you and I have come to know by name was racing down that little dusty path with all her might, so dangerously fast you might have wanted to reach out your hand to slow her down lest she stumble and fall, bounding along as quickly as her trembling legs would carry her, going towards home to tell the others the news she had to tell.

Oh, how I love that scene, carried in the hint of that early dawn, lifted up above herself so much so that it was like her feet never touched the dusty ground; out on that path, with a show of the blue heaven in her eyes, just watch that pretty gal in white, with her shiny black hair streaming behind her in the breeze, flopping back around her brow into her open eyes, which just a moment ago were wet with the tears when she could not find the body of her Lord.

Oh, just watch her over there, lifted on the wings of the morning that she had greeted sometime before the dawn, a fresh new day. Watch her running, bounding, fleeing down the hillside, and listen one last time to the words you need to hear once more. Listen to the shortest, sweetest, loveliest finest little Easter sermon that anyone has ever heard. "Oh, my God," she's saying as she runs. "It's true. He is not dead. He is risen as he said he would. It's true. I saw him. . . I saw him. . . . I looked into his eyes. He lives, and because of him, so shall I live, too. I saw Him. Jesus Christ is risen from the Dead!" Halleluiah, for now and forever more. Amen

BIBLIOGRAPHY OF RELATED READINGS*

Berger, Peter L. *A Rumor of Angels.* New York: Anchor Books, 1970.

Brock, Rita Nakashima and Parker, Rebecca Anne. *Proverbs of Ashes: Violence, Redemptive Suffering, and the Search for What Saves Us.* Boston: Beacon Press, 2002.

Brown, Raymond. *An Introduction to New Testament Christology.* Peabody Massasschusetts: Paulist Press, 1994.

Collins, Robin. *Understanding Atonement: A New and Orthodox Theory.* Available at: http://home.messiah.edu/~rcollins/AT7.HTM.

Craig, William Lane. *Assessing the New Testament Evidence for the Historicity of the Resurrection of Jesus.* Lewiston NY: Mellen Press, 1989.

Crossan, John Dominic. *The Birth of Christianity.* Edinburgh: T &T Clark, 1994.

deChardin, Pierre Teilhard, *The Phenomenon of Man.* New York: Harper and Row, 1955.

Dillard, Annie. *Pilgrim at Tinker Creek.* New York: Harper, 1974.

Dufour, Xavier Leon. *Resurrection and the Meaning of Easter.* Edmonton: G. Chapman, 1974.

Eiseley, Loren C. *All the Strange Hours: The Excavation of a Life.* University of Nebraska Press, 2000.

Ehrman, Bart D. *Lost Christianities.* Oxford: Oxford University Press, 2003.

Ehrman, Bart D. *Lost Scriptures: Books that Did Not make It into the New Testament.* Oxford: Oxford University Press, 2003.

Ehrman, Bart D. *Misquoting Jesus: The Story Behind Who Changed the Bible.* San Francisco: Harper, 2005.

Fuller, Reginald H. *The Formation of the Resurrection Narratives.* Minneapolis: Fortress Press, 1988.

Gopnik, Adam. "Angels and Ages." *The New Yorker,* May 28, 2007, p. 30-37.

Habermas, Gary B. "Resurrection Research from 1975 to the Present: What are Critical Scholars Saying?" *Journal for the Study of the Historical Jesus.* 3.2 (2005). p.135-153.

Hall, Douglas John. *The End of Christendom and the Beginning of Christianity.* Des Moines: Trinity Press International, 1997.

Hennecke, Edgar. *New Testament Apocrypha: Two Volumes.* (Edited by Wilhelm Schneemelcher, Translated by R. McL. Wilson.) Philadelphia: The Westminster Press, 1963.

Jacobovici, Simcha with Pellegrino, Charles, and Cameron, James. *Jesus Family Tomb: The Discovery, the Investigation, and the Evidence That Could Change History.* New York: Harper-Collins, 2007.

Kee, Howard Clark. *The Origins of Christianity: Sources and Documents.* Englewood Cliffs, New Jersey: Prentice-Hall, Inc., 1973.

Malphurs, Aubrey. *A New Kind of Church: Understanding Models of Ministry for the 21st Century.* Grand Rapids: Baker Books, 2007.

McDonald, Lee Martin: *The Biblical Canon: Its Origin, Transmission, and Authority.* Peabody. Massachusetts: Hendrickson Publishers, 2007.

McDonald, Lee Martin and Porter, Stanley E. *Early Christianity and Its Sacred Literature.* Peabody, Massachusetts: Hendrickson Publishers, 2000.

Metzger, Bruce M. *The Canon of the New Testament: Its Origins, Development and Significance.* Oxford: Clarendon Paperbacks, 1997.

Muller, Herbert Joseph. *The Uses of the Past.* Sydney: Galaxy Books, 1963.

Pagels, Elaine and King, Karen L. *Reading Judas: The Gospel of Judas and the Shaping of Christianity.* New York: Viking Penguin, 2007.

Pagels, Elaine. *The Gnostic Gospels.* New York: Random House, 1979.

Perkins, Pheme. *Resurrection: New Testament Witness and Contemporary Reflection.* London: Doubleday, 1984.

Robinson, Anthony. *Transforming Congregational Culture.* Grand Rapids: Eerdmans Publishing Company, 2003.

Robinson, James M. *The Nag Hammadi Library.* Harper San Francisco, 1988.

Sacks, Oliver. *Musicophilia: Tales of Music and the Brain.* New York: Knopf, 2007.

Tabor, James D. *The Jesus Dynasty.* New York: Simon and Shuster, 2006.

Taylor, Barbara Brown. *Leaving Church: A Memoir of Faith.* San Francisco: Harper, 2006.

Teale, Edwin Way. *Wandering Through Winter.* New York: Dodd, Mean & Co., 1965.

The Holy Bible (Revised Standard Version, Second Edition). Iowa Falls: World Book Publishers, 1971

Weaver, J. Denny. *The Non-Violent Atonement.* Grand Rapids: Eerdmans, 2001

Weaver, J. Denny. *Violence in Christian Theology.* CrossCurrents (Internet) Summer 2001, Vol. 51, No. 2.

Williams, H.H. *Resurrection in This Life and the Next.* Oxford: University Press 1963.

* Some of the materials I have in hand are faded carbon copies of original handwritten or hand-typed manuscripts prepared informally for pulpit preaching, Bible studies or speeches, without thought of future publication. I have checked the references as closely as I can, but I fear that the exactitude required in the scholarly fields of theological studies is missing here. I wish that were not so, and I apologize to the reader.

The Author

Dr. Cromie, a native of Pittsburgh, graduated from the University of Pittsburgh and from Pittsburgh Theological Seminary, with honors. He received the Doctor of Philosophy degree in Christian Ethics and Biology from the University of St. Andrews in 1974. He also was awarded a Doctor of Divinity degree from Grove City College in 1980. He has given lectures at Colleges and Seminaries and he has conducted Continuing Education Courses for young ministerial students at Pittsburgh Theological Seminary, Ocean Park Conference Grounds, the Chautauqua Institution in New York, etc.

Dr. Cromie began his ministerial work as a University Pastor for Presbyterian students at Carnegie-Mellon University and the University of Pittsburgh. Following a short time in an inner-city parish ministry in Cleveland, he served on the staff of the historic Shadyside Presbyterian Church in Pittsburgh for six years. Following his studies in St. Andrews, he was pastor of the Parkwood Presbyterian Church in Allison Park, Pennsylvania for three years. From 1973 to 1983 he was Senior Pastor of the Southminster Presbyterian Church in Mt. Lebanon, Pennsylvania. From Pittsburgh Dr. Cromie was called to the First Presbyterian Church of Fort Lauderdale from 1983-1995. For the last decade of his active ministerial work, he was Preaching Pastor at the historic Royal Poinciana Chapel in Palm Beach FL. In 2004 he retired to Matthews NC.

While at Southminster, with the help of some wonderful friends, the Cromies founded Desert Ministries Inc. as a not-for-profit corporation in 1982. Now celebrating its Silver Anniversary, Desert Ministries has distributed 250,000 books and booklets to clergy, laity and churches all over the nation, and Canada and Great Britain. A list of the printed materials available are printed on the next page.

Richard is married to Margaret (Peggy) Good Cromie who is Executive Directress of DMI. They will celebrate their Golden Wedding Anniversary in 2009. They have three children: Catherine Alice Cromie DeCramer who lives in Charlotte with her husband Michael John DeCramer, and their two children Madeline Noel and William Cromie DeCramer (Maddie and Wil); Anne Campbell Cromie, who works with J.K."Buddy" Irby, the Clerk of Courts of Alachua County, Florida, where she also represents the Clerk on the Rape Crisis Center Board in Gainesville FL; and the Rev. Courtney Beth Cromie, Auburn and Princeton Graduate, who is presently an ordained Presbyterian minister at the Yorkminster Presbyterian Church in Yorktown, VA.

Desert Ministries Incorporated

Web site: www. Desmin.org

P.O. Box 747

Matthews NC 28106

Telephone Number: Fax Number

704-849-0901   704-845-1502

Current Publications Available 2007

YOU NOW HAVE CUSTODY OF YOU: Christian Reflections on Marriage and Divorce. by Richard M. Cromie

WHEN YOU LOSE SOMEONE YOU LOVE. by Richard M. Cromie

RELECTIONS ON SUICIDE. by Dr. Perry H. Biddle, Jr.

WHEN ALZHEIMER'S DISEASE STRIKES. by Dr. Stephen Sapp

WHO REALLY LISTENS WHEN I SPEAK? by Jodie Huizenga

THE BEST IS YET TO BE. by Dr. John Calvin Reid

WHEN YOUR LIFE INCLUDES A WHEELCHAIR. by Marilyn Murray Willison

WHEN A CHILD DIES. by Dr. Daniel T. Hans

PRAYERS AGAINST DEPRESSION. by Dr. Lance Martin

A TIME TO MOURN AND A TIME TO DANCE. by Evie McCandless

A JOURNEY THROUGH CANCER. by Dr. Melanie Bone and Dr. Richard M. Cromie

HUMOR AND HEALING. by Dr. Perry H. Biddle, Jr.

DYING WITH GRACE AND HOPE. by Dr. S.Allen Foster

RHAPSODY OF SCRIPTURE. by Dr. Richard M. Cromie

MY COMMITMENT. by Dr. John Calvin Reid

HOW TO HELP AN ALCOHOLIC. by Martin

Sample packets of all of our materials are available
without charge to ministers, churches and study groups.